The Trouble With Evil
Social Control at the Edge of Morality

Edwin M. Lemert

State University of New York Press

Published by
State University of New York Press, Albany

For information, address State University of New York Press,
State University Plaza, Albany, NY 12246

Production by Cynthia Tenace Lassonde
Marketing by Fran Keneston

Library of Congress Cataloging-in-Publication Data

Lemert, Edwin McCarthy, 1912–
    The trouble with evil : social control at the edge of morality /
Edwin M. Lemert.
        p.   cm. — (SUNY series in deviance and social control)
    Includes bibliographical references (p.   ) and index.
    ISBN 0-7914-3243-2 d(hc : alk. paper). — ISBN 0-7914-3244-0 (pb :
alk. paper)
    1. Witchcraft—Africa. 2. Witchcraft—Melanesia. 3. Social
control—Africa. 4. Social control—Melanesia. 5. Good and evil.
6. Africa—Social conditions. 7. Africa—Moral, conditions.
8. Melanesia—Social conditions. 9. Melanesia—Moral conditions.
GN645.L44 1997
306.4'096—dc20   96-30388
                                                                        CIP

10 9 8 7 6 5 4 3 2 1

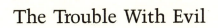

The Trouble With Evil

SUNY series in Deviance and Social Control
Ronald A. Farrell, editor

Contents

Acknowledgments

I wish to thank persons who have taken time to read and comment on the manuscript for this book. These include Michael Petrunik, Carl Sundholm, Hisi Kumagai, and Charles Lemert, all of whom offered useful suggestions as well as encouragement. Special thanks are owed to Michael Winter, who spent time discussing my not always clear ideas and who did yeoman work on the bibliography.

Preface

A fair question for myself to ponder as well as interested others is how or why (or both) I moved from a well-established concern with the field of deviance to the dark and devious subject of evil. In retrospect, after several years of study and writing on the subject, I found it embarrassingly difficult to answer my own question. The need to write a preface for my completed manuscript and some quiet moments of reflection finally cleared my long-term memory enough to recapture the circumstances that led me to persistent thoughts and writing about evil.

It all started with my rereading a book by Carey McWilliams titled *Witch Hunt*. Although the book was hortatory in tone, it nevertheless impressed me as a worthy documentation of the politics of heresy in a democratic society stressed by the Cold War.

Later a book simply called *Inquisition*, published in 1991 and written by Carlton Sherwood, a Pulitzer Prize winner, awakened my interest in the larger subject of evil, particularly the witch hunt. This the author described with richly documented detail in a chapter of seventy-five pages. It and other chapters related in fine detail the persecution and prosecution of the Reverend Sun Myung Moon and his accountant for income tax evasion. This was contrived by a very purposeful attorney implausibly (or perhaps plausibly) named Martin Flumenbaum in a regional office of the Department of Justice.

The two books in question gave me the idea that witch hunts might be more than adventitious historical events, and that they might be conceived as manifestations of universal processes of social control. With this in mind I forthwith undertook to gain some mastery of historical materials on the European Inquisition. This project fired my interest in large-scale witch hunts for a year or more until I realized how difficult it would be to extract some common pattern from the divergent data turned up from countless sources by the busy historians. A chance encounter with a historian friend on our faculty confirmed my doubts that as yet no consistent theory or interpretation had surfaced in the growing sea of literature on the European Inquisition. To cap the matter, and to my relief, I suddenly recalled a statement by an early mentor that history seldom provides sufficient information to answer questions put by sociologists.

Meantime I had found and read Evans-Pritchard's (1937) diligent record of witchcraft among the Azande people of Africa. I was struck by his proposal that their witchcraft was a "prototype of evil . . . a planned assault of one man on another . . . with malice aforethought." For quite a while thereafter I read and wrote with a scheme in mind in which the prototype of evil would serve for the analysis of political witch hunts in modern societies as well as primitive.

Unfortunately the data on witch hunts in different areas of Africa could not be easily applied either to the European Inquisition or to the modern political witch hunt conceived by McWilliams. Sadly I moved on to a more limited objective—a comparative study of witchcraft and sorcery in Africa and Melanesia. For a while the chapter on the witch hunt dangled in the book outline until I realized that its proper place was following the chapter on African sorcery and witchcraft, for the simple reason that witchcraft rather than sorcery was the predominant mystical belief/ritual to be found there.

One way to perceive my book is as a series of essays loosely connected by their focus on evil in primitive societies. This, however, overlooks its dominant emphasis on social control, which is made problematical by tenuous leadership structures, the ambiguities of evil, and conflicting cultural values.

Chapter 1 of the book reviews the sporadic attempts of sociologists to define evil in abstract terms. While these are inventive and informative efforts, they reflect more virtuosity than data and sustainable theory development. More recently a few sociologists have written in passing about evil as transcendence, and one large study seeks to demonstrate that crime is evil by reference to its concomitant emotions. Generally speaking, I believe that while sociological writings may have some relevance to the question of evil, they lack materiality.

Chapter 2 of the book provides a working term for evil but not a definition. This follows Karl Lewellyn's idea that one need not define subject matter in order to study it and that there may be disadvantages to so doing. Evil as experience is a simple idea that while persons cannot readily articulate what evil is, they can nevertheless be acutely aware of its presence in the form of intense fear and the pressure for action. Empirically the presence of evil connotes negative feelings; but as the Melanesian data show, this may be a cultural bias.

Chapter 3 discusses evil in several cultures but with the main emphasis on those in Africa. Early ethnographers there worked under the self-imposed theoretical stricture of a kind of "structuralist orthodoxy," which ultimately gave way to the idea of process analysis.

Chapter 4 describes and analyzes the witch hunt as a form of social control in the colonial setting of Africa. This kind of social movement did not appear in Melanesia, where the response to social change took the form of cargo cults. Witch hunts originated as dispersed movements that evolved around charismatic leaders and became forerunners of nationalistic agitation to come.

Chapter 5 is titled Evil and Social Control in Melanesia in deference to the great differentiation of cultures there. A common feature of the cultures throughout the area is the reliance on shaming as a means of social control. Equally important in understanding social control throughout Melanesia is the salient social value of equivalence, which has widespread implications for social control through personal leadership.

Chapter 7 of the work is a conclusion that strives to draw together the strands of meaning and theory that have come to light from the study of the ethnographic materials bearing on witchcraft and sorcery mainly in Africa and Melanesia.

1

The Sociological Perspective on Evil

My purpose in the writings that follow is to discuss whether evil can be subjected to sociological analysis and, more precisely, whether it can be studied with the existing methods of social science as an extension of the study of deviance and social control. Put as a query, I ask whether our understanding of deviance can be deepened or broadened by the inclusion of evil as part of its subject matter. In short, does the study of evil help complete the sociological account of what happens when there is deviance.

For some sociologists, perhaps most, such questions will appear to be regressive, or a circling back to an earlier era of thinking when a number of writers more or less took the existence of evil for granted. I refer here to turn-of-the-century books of social reformers in which they wrote of the "social evils," such as prostitution, gambling, and drunkenness, sometimes explicitly attributing the latter to the "demon rum."

In contrast to these writings, those of persons identified with the social science movement of the post–Civil War period reflected growing commitment to the philosophy of the early physical and biological sciences that rejected explanations of human behavior based on other than natural phenomena. The ascendancy of rationalism as the underlying premise of Western thought became so complete that references to supernatural explanations of events by social scientists were likely to put them at risk professionally.

There are particular reasons why present-day sociologists have avoided the topic of evil, apart from their allegiance to the rigors of the scientific method and its associated philosophy of

1

positivism. One is the prevalence of cultural relativism as a predominant perspective. An extension of this is the reluctance of sociologists openly to apply terms like "bad," "immoral," or "evil" except in descriptive or analytical contexts. Sociologists often have been at their best playing the role of the demystifier or the unmasker, who exposes the dilapidation and gaps between moral principles and human action. In so doing at times they have dealt heavily in irony and paradox, especially in discussions of deviance. Finally, sociologists have excluded possible concern with evil by conceiving social control and deviance in terms of rules, rule compliance, and conformity, which while relevant to the study of bureaucratized society, scarcely allow comprehension of morality and evil in a broader universalistic sense.

Despite the formidable hindrances to the enterprise, a small number of sociologists have boldly confronted the subject of evil both as a substantive issue as well as analytical. Among the very first, if not the first, sociologists to write on evil as a distinctive topic was E. A. Ross, whose work *Sin and Society* appeared in 1907. For Ross (p. 98), evil was essentially the equivalent of sin, something he defined as "conduct which harms another." Sin, he said, is not self-limiting, as is the case with vice; hence, "Satan's main onset today is on the side of sin rather than vice."

However outdated the post-Victorian Ross's words sound today, nevertheless, his empirical referents for sin were surprisingly modern, being directed at the lack of accountability and control of corporations—a condition that, he said, "transmits the greed of investors but not their conscience" (p. 102). Seeking to fashion a corporate morality, he spoke of monopoly as a "fiduciary sin," along with such practices as rebates, dummy directors, flaunting of factory laws, insurance thievery, inoperative mine inspection laws, and laws for tenement reform.

Ross was essentially a social critic/reformer perturbed by the depredations of the so-called robber barons of the time and their large-scale business and industrial combinations. In a sense his tactics were like those of General Custer's, who "rode to the sound of the guns." His theoretical premises came from French social psychology, which opposed the individual to society as "anti-social" and needing socialization into its fabric. Like some of the other sociologists of his time, he was little deterred from designating evil and evildoers as he saw them and urging their social control.

More than half a century passed before any sociologist appeared in print to argue for the creation of a sociology of evil. The first such publications in what might be called the modern era were written by Kurt Wolff for Italian and French journals (1964, 1967); his English statement came in 1969, "For a Sociology of Evil," published in a psychological rather than a sociological journal. Among other concerns Wolff stressed the need to study alienation and the misdirection Weber's (1958) idea of a value-free society had given to sociology.

In 1978 came the first lengthy discourse on evil *per se* by Stanford Lyman: *The Seven Deadly Sins: Society and Evil.* While the background rationale in this, and to a lesser extent in Wolff's papers, did not exclude concern with the corporate misdoings condemned as evil by Ross, it nevertheless changed to reflect existentialist misgivings about the mission of sociology itself and to feature the alienated nature of the human condition engendered by a corporate-based world. Thus Lyman charged sociology with lacking an awareness and a language for confronting the ubiquitous erosion of meaning resulting from the rationalizing, "scientizing," and bureaucratizing of human activity.

Lyman (1978, viii) does not match Ross's crisp definition of sin. Rather he stated that "Evil is let loose whenever the capacity to criticize is subverted." He then calls evil a "structure of alienating sins." The reader must then find definitions or delineations for each of the seven deadly sins in succeeding chapters of the book, some of which are clear, some necessarily ambiguous.

Overall a reader of *The Seven Deadly Sins*, although likely to be enchanted by the author's lyrical style and erudition, is left uncertain as to his intent. One cannot tell whether the writer is claiming the existence of an objective standard of good by which evil can be judged or merely describing social dramas of good and evil with the implied need to look behind the dramas to decipher true evil. This may follow from a reluctance by Lyman to abandon his "sociology of the absurd" perspective (1989), or it may simply be the inability to rise above one of the salient features Lyman attributes to the "mood" of modern dramas of evil, namely its ambiguity.

A heady conclusion from reading *The Seven Deadly Sins* is that the closer one gets to the subject of evil, the finer its analysis, the more ambiguous it becomes. As I will try to show, this inheres in the process of its ascription and the sociocultural context out of which any formulation or imputation of evil comes.

Other attributes of emergent evil in modern society that have been recognized by sociologists are those of scale and impersonality. They acquire their meaning from the large numbers of Jews and ethnic minorities put to death by German Nazis in World War II and cases of wholesale massacres of civilians during the Viet Nam War. Everett Hughes (1971, 1962) contended with the question, somewhat obliquely put, why otherwise "good" people in Germany tolerated the operation of the death camps. In answer to his own question he concluded that the problem revolved around "dirty work" and implied that in various forms and degrees it exists in all societies. It exists because ordinary people avoid thinking and talking about such things lest group solidarity be threatened. Moreover the greater the social distance between ordinary people and those the object of dirty work, the more likely an implicit mandate will be given to those who carry it out, in this case persons who are isolated from groups other than their own. Hughes also stated that dirty work people tend to be social failures.

Whether Nazi organizations and administration of the holocaust were staffed primarily by social failures or evil people is a debatable point, considering the wide variety of workers. Non-Germans and victims themselves, including Jews, worked in collecting, transporting, and killing victims of the holocaust. Beyond this is the nagging question of whether persons playing roles and obeying directives in large-scale organizations can be shown to work by evil intent or to commit manifestly evil acts. This is the painful theme encountered in Hannah Arendt's (1965, p. 287) study of the Eichman trial in Israel, which she subtitled *A Report on the Banality of Evil*:

> when I speak of the banality of evil, I do so only on a
> strictly factual level, pointing to a phenomenon which

stared one in the face at the Eichman trial. Eichman was not Iago and not Macbeth, and nothing would have been farther from his mind to determine with Richard III, "to prove a villain."

Lewis Coser (1969), who was equally concerned with Nazi genocidal projects, proposed a somewhat different solution to Hughes's query about the tolerance of evil by presumably good people. This was "structured visibility," which hides or protects people from sensual overload. He posited the existence of limits to the "span of sympathy" ordinary people have for remote victims of evil. Finally, Coser offered the idea that apocalyptic evil of such massive scope implies that victims "must have done something" to deserve such treatment. However, he does not tell us whether such reactions are themselves evil, merely how they make evil possible.

Sanctions for Evil

What Hughes, Coser, and some other sociologists were saying is that, given certain circumstances and beliefs, almost any human being is capable of ignoring, minimizing, or tolerating the evil practices of others. In a somewhat different way, Arendt specified how evil can result from the dispassionate, workaday motivations and ambitions of bureaucrats. A line of thought less passive than that of the sensory-removed audience and the mindless bureaucrat runs through another publication of a group of social scientists that includes sociologists, namely *Sanctions for Evil* (1971). This develops a common theme that doers of evil actually are sanctioned by other members of society who negatively evaluate and dehumanize other groups of people.

Among the sociologists contributing to the volume, Smelser (1971) somewhat legalistically defined evil as the use of coercion, force, and violence that exceeds institutional or legal "limits," or their use by persons without authority to do so. The result is destructiveness. A condition necessary for such an eventuality is a belief that some enemy is evil, intelligent, and omnipotent. At the same time the perpetrator of evil holds to a belief in his own omnipotence and moral superiority. Illustrations are Christian militancy, Nazism, and vigilantism. Precipitation of evil follows from its legitimation, authorization, and rationalization.

Granting its conceptual symmetry, the most that can be concluded from all of this is that evil (read destructiveness) is the outcome of the process of collective behavior and group conflict. It remains unclear as to what is gained by introducing the term evil into such analysis, especially since the author gives no standard for determining what the limits of force are. Similarly no standard is given for judging the meaning of "unauthorized" actions involving destruction, such as the Boston Tea Party by revolutionary Americans.

Troy Duster (1971), by assuming that the absence of guilt is necessary for evil action, outlines a hypothetical state that, in the manner of Garfinkel's (1956) "Conditions of Successful Degradation Ceremonies," proposes "Conditions of a Guilt Free Massacre." He sets down six such conditions, ranging from public faith in the organizational arm of violence, downgrading of individual grounds for action, fragmentation of distributive responsibility in organizations, secrecy, a vulnerable population, and developing a motivation for massacre.

Duster somewhat perversely raises but does not answer the questions about the corporate responsibility for destructive actions. He leaves the issue unclear as to whether groups can experience guilt or be held guilty. In sum he merely shows how a number of people can be shown to have massacred others without a pronouncement of guilt or a sense of guilt in the acting persons. While Duster's piece is a plausible enough formulation, whether it fits the actual history of massacres, he does not question nor even discuss. Off hand a significant exception comes to mind in the massacres of White settlers by Native Americans, who were highly individualistic in war-making and without much if any corporate organization in Duster's sense of the term.

A somewhat more Olympian sociological analysis of evil by Robert Bellah (1971) looks to the communal foundations of American society in a search for the sanctions for evil. These he finds in intrapsychic repression connected with the exclusion or rejection of some groups by others, originally on simple religious grounds, later in history on the high moral grounds of religious piety, and finally on the basis of economic success or failure. Bellah readily admits that all societies have a "dialectic of inclusion and exclusion" but argues that this can be overcome by creating a new open society and a "new man." Bellah is forgiving towards the principals in the killing of villagers in the Viet Nam War, allowing that "we too might have acted as they did." However, not so for those who "failed to create punitive sanctions" and take action against the evildoers.

A conclusion from the writings of sociologists so far cited is that they tend to take the nature of evil for granted or see it broadly as harm or destructiveness. As such, evil emerges as a product of universalistic intrapsychic processes associated with group identities and the projection of primitive aspects of the person onto scapegoat groups. The concomitant destructiveness is "sanctioned," abetted, or even forgiven by humanization, fragmented responsibility, sensual overload, low visibility, or by lack of sanctions against evil acts.

While these sociologists concerned with evil do not quite endow man the social animal with original sin, they make it clear that given certain sociopsychological circumstances he is prone to evil—a kind of "there but for the grace of God go I" perception or one of "it could happen to anyone." In a paradoxical way they are caught up in the positivism of conventional methods of analysis, and, by finding causes for given behavior, inescapably mitigate the evil they identify and decry. They humanize that which has to be dehumanized to be evil. In so doing, however sophisticated their approaches, they do little to dispel the cloud of ambiguity that has hung over the subject for centuries.

The Roots of Evil

I prolong my critical search of the sociological literature on evil to include the work of Ervin Laub (1989), *The Roots of Evil*, who, although writing from a psychological vantage point, incorporates a variety of societal, cultural, and group concepts in his comparative study of mass killings. This has the special merit of concentrating on data with a known provenance from which relevant concepts are derived. As the title of the book suggests, Laub writes with an eye to the moral history or evolution of human violence in its collective aspects. Laub says that individuals have potentialities for good and for evil, likewise groups. The direction they take is influenced by various factors: economic hardship, nationalism, ideology, motivations of perpetuators and bystanders, cultural self-concepts, and others.

Laub concedes that evil is not a scientific concept and that it has no agreed-on meaning, but that the idea of evil is part of the human heritage. A *non sequitur* nevertheless follows: "the essence of evil is the destruction of human beings." Added to this is the idea that the evil of group violence has a potential for growth much like a geometrical progression. In common with sociologists previously cited, Laub has some logical difficulties with the relationship of individual and group motivation but overrides these by saying that groups are like individuals so far as the optional development of good and evil is conceded.

Starkly considered, Laub's work does little more than append the term evil to its title and make some passing contextual references to it. It is, properly seen, a study of mass killings, defensible and praiseworthy as scholarship, but not as an understanding of evil. While an admitted feature of evil is incomprehensibility, Laub obviously believed that it can be made comprehensible. Thus he, along with sociologists, knowingly or unknowingly removed part of its core meaning.

Evil as Transcendence

Two sociologists have moved perceptibly away from broad causational explanations of evil to focus on its special sociopsychological concomitants as they relate to deviance and crime. In so doing they reflect ideas traceable to philosophy and literature, particularly French literature, that revolve around problems of validating human existence and repairing attenuated identity.

Shoham (1979) in his work *Salvation Through the Gutters*, draws heavily on psychodynamic psychology and myths along with ideas from Nietzsche to account for the evil dimensions of human acts. Such deviance is transcendental or heroic in nature and follows from "ontological prodding of the self" in persons whose lives are devoid of meaning and reality. Negative acts, such as murder or arson, because of their basic ontological significance, give structure, meaning, or social substance to eroded identity. "Playing evil roles" in this way becomes an act of self-definition.

The theme of Shoham's work, figuratively put in the title of his book, was among other things influenced by the literature now grown to legendary proportions surrounding the life of Jean Genet. Genet and his varied literary chroniclers more or less colluded to fashion a grand moral paradox or ethical inversion in which "betrayal, theft, and homosexuality" are converted into saintliness, allegedly due to the intensity and purity of motivation to pursue such actions. Genet thus sought to glorify depravity as a means to achieve a sense of sovereignty, to transcend his low status and spoiled identity as defined by ordinary moral standards.

Genet's depiction (Dort, 1979) of his emergent superdeviant motivations stands as a delight to remaining partisans of labeling theory:

> In order to weather my desolation, when I withdrew more deeply into myself. I worked out inadvertently a rigorous discipline I have used ever since. So to every charge brought against me, unjust though it were, from the bottom of my heart I would answer "guilty." No sooner had I pronounced the word or phrase signifying it, when I myself felt the need to become what I had been accused of being.

Shoham incorporates such material on Genet into a kind of existentialist explanation of deviance resulting from separation of the ego from others and the resultant striving for congruence between them. This takes the author on a wide-ranging discussion of the works of Jung and neo-Freudians, as well as of religion, philosophy, and criminology. There is little systematic use of empirical data in the discussions.

Crime as Doing Evil

The most striking and in many ways captivating challenge to conventional studies of crime appeared with Katz's (1988) volume on *Seductions of Crime* subtitled *The Moral and Sensual Attractions of Evil*. If the author does not fly in the face of positivist criminology, he certainly grievously faults it for its sins of omission. In essence he claims that prevailing studies of crime are insufficient or poorly grounded. They lack empirical substance, primarily because they ignore "Evil . . . as lived in everyday realities of society"(p. 10).

However, evil *per se* is less featured in Katz's discussions than the subjective states or "foreground factors" which accompany, precede, or induce various crimes by reason of their seductive qualities. These vary depending on the nature of the crime subjected to analysis, consisting of "sneaky thrills," "magic of violence," "transcendence on the field," "sovereignty," "spirit of street elites," "transcendent fascinations," "moral dominance" or "moral advantage," "moral meanness," "dizzying moral emotions," and "cosmological control."

Katz stretches his term for evil considerably when he speaks of inspiring dread as "moral advantage" (p. 88 ff) gained by threat and violence. In his descriptions these sound much more like simple intimidation, menace, open defiance, or provocation. However, such characteristics are scarcely applicable to the "thrills" experienced by teenage shoplifters, since there is little or no interaction between them and their proprietary victims. Intimidation practiced by "street elites" on the other hand obviously requires victims or an audience. Likewise, "doing stickup" robbery by its nature requires victims as well as specific kinds of situations. But here there may be a technical or instrumental need for dominance in the sense of using skilled threats to obtain money or other valuables. Katz, however, argues in some detail against the stumbling block idea that robbers evolve their techniques rationally to any significant degree.

Katz properly calls attention to the importance of feelings, emotions, and nuances of meaning important to the commission of some but not all forms of crime, especially as they bear on the subjective needs of offenders which are satisfied by their violent actions. Many of these concomitants are implicit rather than explicit and have to be inferred from analysis of cases. Katz alleges (p. 11) to have used the method of analytic induction for this purpose but unfortunately gives only his results rather than demonstrating stepwise his use of data in a critical fashion.

It is possible to apply alternative explanations to Katz's material on stickups by Blacks. One of these directs attention to the situational particulars of such crimes. A goodly proportion of the victims of robberies and robbery-homicides are known to the offender and occur in residences; likewise the two in many cases live in close proximity to one another. Such facts are consistent with Donald Black's (1983) theory of crime as social control in which offenders seek to redress specific wrongs done them by particular others.

It is true that Katz employs the concept of social control but primarily as a dramatic act by an offender to assert control over the chaos in his personal life, who like Shakespeare's protagonist "takes arms against a sea of troubles and by opposing seeks to end them." What Katz fails to explore is that the stickup offender in his reaction to chaos may be opting for the specific negative identity of jail or prison inmate by the seeming irrational manner in which he performs the crime. He may be responding to high stress levels that ultimately go with his "hardman" image or identity.

In such a case, maintaining the hardman identity grows unbearable not only because of stress but because the rewards of stickup over time lose their validating effects for the self. Katz inadvertently recognized this when he noted the instance of a harassed robber who expressed relief on his arrest and by citing Laurie Taylor's (1984, p. 180) observation from English research that some such "villains" at critical points harbor a death wish so that they deliberately increase their visibility and thereby the likelihood of detection. These interpretations clearly are not consistent with the idea that the stickup man is imposing "disciplined control" by force of his personality over his chaotic life situation. Rather he is openly engineering a change of identity as an escape from his present life situation.

All of this reflects an underlying problem with Katz's type of analysis in that he sees transcendence as a state or a condition that explains criminal acts. His analysis is synchronic rather than diachronic and overlooks the possibility now entertained by some writers (Olson & Rouner, 1981; Griffin, 1991) that transcendence must be seen as a process, or possibly as part of a process. Thus the same actions may have different meanings at different stages of a process or of a criminal career. Unless this is known, a kind of time or "phase" bias may affect case history data.

In my older study (Lemert, 1972) of systematic check forgers I found that they moved through a cycle of rising stress coupled with declining satisfaction with their "fast" life style composed of indulgence in fine clothes, first-class air travel, staying at fine hotels, gambling, and intercourse with women available on short acquaintance. Mounting stress came from the ubiquitous threat of arrest, while declining life satisfaction resulted from compounding social isolation imposed by the forger's high mobility, use of false identities, and closely guarded interpersonal interaction precluding the intimate validation of self. Finally, identity itself eroded to a point of crisis, at which time arrest usually occurred. This allowed reidentification in socially realistic, albeit negative, terms.

At the time I did this research and writing I realized that the robber's ultimate problem was analogous to that of the committed check forger in that both become isolated, although for different reasons. Further study may very well reveal that the robber's reputation as a hardman or as "somewhat crazy" (Katz's term) gets fed by his intimidation of personal associates as well as by his crime victims; this, complicated by his violent treatment of women, magnifies his social isolation and alienation in his own world. Thus while it emerges in a different context, critical social isolation of the stickup criminal may have the effect of precipitating an identity crisis much as it does for the systematic check forger.

The brief comparisons I have drawn here between stickup criminals and systematic check forgers necessarily raise questions about the sufficiency of the concept of transcendence as an explanation of evil. There are certainly "sensual dynamics" associated with bad checks passing in the form of thrills, excitement, and gamelike exhilaration that qualify as transcendence. However, ordinarily there is no visible "moral advantage" over victims as with stickups because the bogus nature of the bad checks is discovered only later. Nor does the crime produce violence; check forgers seldom if ever possess weapons and, in interviews, protest that they "could never hurt anyone." With passing time the check forger's active criminal life does not become chaotic so much as empty and meaningless.

Although transcendence is a recognizable aspect of the check forger's criminal experience, he does not typically have an antecedent illicit life style attributed by Katz to street elites, "bad ass niggers," and stickup criminals. According to my early findings, habitual check criminals often came from middle-class backgrounds and in some cases were highly educated. A final dissenting note is that while such criminals may have been attracted "sensually" to bogus check passing, they did not find it morally seductive; to the contrary they were typically perplexed and deeply perturbed by the moral contradictions between their crimes and their conventional upbringing.

From what I have said and what research likely would show, transcendence can be the concomitant of a number of different crimes that vary greatly in the extent to which they can be characterized as evil. Moreover the need for transcendence may be a secondary effect of a crime as well as a cause, a confusion best eliminated by following some form of process or extended, trouble case analysis.

Common knowledge grants that transcendence is not exclusively a feature of evil crimes; it occurs in the lives of conventionally moral persons. Mystical experiences happen to people making up the normal population in many cultures and, as William James (1977) wrote, are institutionalized as religious expression. Artists and musicians attest to "moments of truth" in their creative moods; linebackers on professional football teams are known to "go a little crazy" prior to game time, yet revert to peaceful family life afterwards. Indeed even professors may transcend their sedate milieus, as in the case of Erving Goffman, whom Bennett Berger (1971, p. 136) referred to as pursuing his observations and writings with "demonic detachment."

While Katz fathered a host of fresh ideas for the study of crime, he made no effort and did little to clarify the idea of evil; if anything, like others writing on the topic, he has added ambiguity to the term. A pertinent query is why he chose to use the word in the title of his book and intermittently in his discussions, for in likelihood they could have been put just as well without invoking the notion of evil. Questions of this sort turn attention to the author's purpose in writing his book, his mission, if you will, and to the audience he addresses, as well as to the larger purpose he conveyed by his writing style. It shifts attention away from evil *per se* to its rhetoric.

The Rhetoric of Evil

Lyman's writings on sin and evil stirred little lasting interest among sociologists or among those in its most relevant area, deviance and criminology; but in one respect they were ahead of their time. I refer to his urgent call for a rhetoric of evil. As he put the matter (1978, viii):

> we lack a rhetoric of criticism for social evils . . . a rhetoric that grasps the structures of consciousness, the phenomenology of history and the dramaturgy of contemporary scenes. . . . Such a new rhetoric . . . would take evil as a topic in its own right, seeking to uncover its historical backgrounds, describe its social forms and architectonics, and examine its supports and strengths.

It is only recently that sociologists and researchers in the field of communications have given a "new turn" to rhetoric or returned to its study with new perspectives. In the past, rhetoric suffered ill repute among scientists, who often treat it with derision or as an antithesis to logic, reason, and objective communication. Current rhetorical studies, while focusing on how best to persuade an interested, informed, and judicious audience, now analyze written and oral materials to decipher how they are qualified and given epiphenomenal meaning by their format and style (Simon, 1989; Hunter, 1990).

Gusfield (1988, 1987, 1981), for example, portrayed how a kind of special rhetoric develops as part of the culture of social problems, such as drunk driving, but was content merely to point to its deficiencies. Lyman (1978) seemingly is the only sociologist self-consciously to undertake the task of creating a rhetoric of evil. Whether he succeeded is dubious, and if he did, it was a fractured rhetoric.

A careful reading of Lyman's discussion of the various sins of mankind shows that he employed two vocabularies, one historical and morally descriptive, another conceptualizing such things as overeating, addiction to drugs, and alcoholism with terms taken from texts on deviance and abnormal psychology. The "rhetoric" appears in captions that combine the two vocabularies, such as Gluttony and Social Structure, The Social Construction of Gluttony, and Absolution from the Sin of Gluttony: Strategies of Excuse and Justification. [See ch. 6] The text itself is threaded with sermonizing frequently in the manner of Old Testament prophets, fittingly conveyed by the last word in his book, "Amen."

Evil as Metatext

Lyman's lone voice on the subject does not mean that sociological compositions are so sanitized by the scienific method as to be barren of any reference to evil, nor indeed, that scientific writing more generally avoids the attractions of evil—to loosely use Katz's phrase. Quite a few years ago Merton (1949) and later Kuhn (1962) demonstrated that science has a moral structure that is affected by social influences, and that scientists tend to accept or reject ideas and findings based on their congruence with paradigms legitimized in their fields. A good deal of discussion in the scientific field thus takes the form of strategic debates over the moral validity of assumptions, definitions, models, and perspectives (Toulmin, 1958).

Insofar as the human sciences are in a preparadigmatic stage or in a state of unresolved conflicting perspectives, much of the writing follows a persuasive mode rather than one of logical proof. Authors in these instances play the role of rhetor or animator as well as that of scientist, and they complicate their tests by introducing elements of multivocality and polyphony. This can be done through the use of epigraphs, metaphors, and allusions, and the restatement of opposing views in captions—all of which serve in varying degrees as a metatext.

The metatext of evil on close scrutiny may be no more than implicit in the way in which discussions are framed. Whether referents of evil are implicit or explicit, they track discussion at a level of the unprovable, the contingent, the uncertain, and the judgmental. The rhetoric of evil more than any other draws upon the "resources of ambiguity" in language because it touches and activates deeply rooted emotions and dialectical forms of thought.

La Piere (1938) pointed this out many years ago in his work on *Collective Behavior* in which he attributed a "universal habit of human thinking about group conflict." This he saw as a contest between heroes and villains. Nor did La Piere hold scholarly lecturers immune from this tendency to dramatize issues as persons in conflict in order to motivate their audiences. One way this is done is to dramatize deviance as a "social problem story . . . [that] is simply a tragedy in which the system is made out to be the villain" (p. 243).

More recently a somewhat similar point of view surfaced in assertions that rhetorically considered, classical sociology variously depicts human societies as being in a state of vague malaise that needs explanation. For example, Davis (1986) contends that the seductive appeal of such theories lies in their ambiguity that allows the authors to play on the fears of readers. Each classic writer (Marx, Durkheim, Freud and Weber) regarded his fundamental factor—(alienation, unresolved Oedipal conflict, the division of labor or anomie, and rationality) as a "major source of evil in the modern world to the degree that it undermines the individual and society."

A current author, Stivers (1982), goes even further, by insisting that sociology in general harbors a concealed rhetoric of evil. This he attributes to the high technological development of American society and its displacement of rhetoric by media propaganda. In the process the social sciences have supplanted religion as sources of moral discourse. One way positivist sociology does this is by symbolizing evil as a social problem. In subsequent analysis Stivers confines himself to a limited study of deviance, namely the violation of sacred rules whose transgression makes up the content of evil. Presumably this is revealed in modern myths and rituals that symbolize order and chaos of social life. While there is a laudable ingenuity in all of this, it is doubtful that the data of folk beliefs and the tenuous interpretations of structuralism are entirely adequate to clarify evil in our highly secularized society.

Even if what Stivers says about the positivists is true, it does not follow that in all instances they are loath to employ a rhetoric of evil openly in arguments for superiority of hard science methodology. Whether this is done without complicity or is a product of an inner Mephistophelean bargain is a question best left to the reader.

An instructive case of explicit utilization of rhetorical evil comes down from the annals of social problems literature, namely, in Hirschi's 1973 article on "Procedural Rules and the Study of Deviant Behavior." In retrospect this piece has always struck me as the thinly disguised polemic of an indignant positivist with a rhetorical no-tricks-barred stance, girded to do battle with the proponents of the then-dominant labeling theory of deviance and crime. The author's strategy targeted a number of methodological rules which, he averred, had arisen outside of science to serve unscientific needs and were destined to interfere with the sociological enterprise. These had become oral traditions of the deviance field and the hidden agenda of graduate instruction.

Hirschi imputed his list of rules to a kind of contraculture methodology, headed by the injunction to avoid the "evil causes evil fallacy." Under this are to be found both upbeat and downbeat headings, such as "seek evil explanations of good phenomena," and near the bottom of them all, one highly provocative to the author, "appreciate deviance." This he likened to the "happy nigger" theory of race relations.

It is not difficult to find La Piere's (1938) good guys and bad guys in Hirschi's article. The bad guys are labeling theorists, who used nontheory and antitheory to undermine and threaten sociology with destruction. The good guys continued to defend "traditional" or "conventional" logic and methods, with heed to empirical evidence as the final arbiter of theoretical validity.

The puzzle here is why did Hirschi choose to paraphrase his argument with the rhetoric of evil. Ostensibly this was a reaction to the use of the same rhetoric by those he opposed, the bad guys, in this instance Cohen (1970) and Matza (1969). Presumably Hirschi opted to meet them on their own ground and accepted evil metaphorically as a choice of weapons. Still more attractive to Hirschi, perhaps, was the opportunity to demonstrate virtuosity in determining whether the "liberal" deviance-loving proponents of science unruly labeling theory had any moral concerns at all. This was apparent in one passage of the article in which Hirschi, while denying the validity of the good-causes-evil hypothesis, nevertheless stated that if he had to choose between it and the evil-causes-evil hypothesis he would certainly choose evil. This certainly clouds, if not reverses, his earlier disclaimer that he did not want to defend evil.

While none would associate Hirschi, a leading figure in the field of criminology, with evil, nevertheless in this instance his arguments did reveal an impish quality. If evil *per se* held no attractions for Hirschi the same cannot be said for its rhetoric, which here obviously had a seductive appeal.

Is There a Prototype of Evil

From what has been written so far and more that could be written, it is fair to say that human beings, including sociologists, appear to have a need for a language, rhetoric, and even a belief in the existence of evil. This is a precarious point of departure for discussion in that it invites reification and tautology, saying that because people widely recognize evil there must be a need to do so. It also entangles thinking in shopworn structural or structure/function social theory, in essence that, given said needs, institutional forms arise to satisfy the needs and merge into a self-renewing system.

The difficulty with such theory is that real-life people have to develop such institutions, meaning that they must first recognize their "need," make choices to do something about it, get themselves organized, and discover the means to do so. But alas, people do not always do this—sometimes they mistake their need, or they make the wrong choices, or they find the effort too great, or they simply lack the means to pursue their purposes. Sometimes people do without cultural techniques that might make their lives more convenient, fulfilling, and free of anxiety. Sometimes they get carried away by their ideas and beliefs and devise patterns of action that create more problems than they solve. This may be especially true of evil insofar as it is a product of the efforts to exterminate it.

It is with these caveats in mind that I return to the captional query above as to the existence of a prototype of evil. This concept comes from older field research initiated by Evans-Pritchard (1968) on witchcraft among the Azande people in Southern Sudan. This study along with Kluckhohn's (1944, p. 107) work on Navaho witchcraft has figured prominently among anthropological discussions of magic, sorcery, and witchcraft. Evans-Pritchard termed Azande witchcraft a prototype of evil because it was: "A planned assault by one man on another . . . a witch acts with malice aforethought . . . hatred, jealousy, envy, backbiting and slander go ahead and witchcraft follows after. A man must hate his enemy then bewitch him."

Evans-Pritchard's discussion of Azande witchery makes it clear that he spoke of belief only and that, as the Azande described it, no actual witchcraft existed among them. Nevertheless he regarded their beliefs and associated rituals as a prototype of evil because they pervaded the whole fabric of Azande society; they were the focus of ethical beliefs and the central fact of social control. People attributed all misfortunes as well as personal wrongs where the perpetrators were unknown, such as adultery, to witchcraft. Witchcraft, when "discovered," demanded vengeance.

Both Evans-Pritchard and Kluckhohn sought functionalist explanations of witchcraft: as a natural philosophy to account for misfortune, as an outlet for aggression, to affirm group solidarity by socially defining the "bad" or "malevolent," and for social control through scapegoating. It was also a means of gaining wealth and securing women, disposing of enemies, and gaining "center stage" for low-ranking persons. The two studies of witchcraft, along with a number of other mid-century studies of African witchcraft, revolved theoretically around structural concerns, or to use Kluckhohn's term (1944, p. 60), "structural dynamics." This, among other things, had to do with lineage stresses, their growth and decline, the power and affluence of chiefdoms, and maintenance of respect for elders affecting and affected by witchcraft.

The two notable early studies and some of the later studies, while highly informative and allowing comparisons, failed to generate cumulative replications, despite the attention they gave to social structures. The differences and inconsistencies brought to light in field studies of witchcraft in a number of African societies make the claim for the existence of a prototype difficult to sustain. Although Evans-Pritchard disinguished witchcraft from sorcery and magic among the Azande, the distinctions did not hold for other African societies. Nor did the apparent absence of the political use of sorcery hold true for other African peoples, as for example, among the Basuto in the first part of the nineteenth century when ritual murder and sorcery were practiced for purposes of political advancement (Jones, 1951).

Gluckman (1965) noted in a commentary that the Azande recently had been relocated by the Sudan government at the time of Evans-Pritchard's study, which may have accounted for their unusual pattern of lacking accusations of witchcraft within the lineal kinship group of the Azande.

Evans-Pritchard offered only passing references to the reactions of the Azande to colonial laws that forbade vengeance killings and compensation damages for witchcraft. This in retrospect was an unfortunate omission, in the light of reactions attributed to East African natives among whom such laws generated social tensions, leading them to believe that the State had aligned itself on the side of evil.[1]

Another difficulty that denies easy acceptance of the Azandes' witchcraft as a generic model for evil is the apparently minimal influence of religious beliefs in relation to witchcraft. On this point Harwood (1970) challenged the model, based on his comparisons with the Safwa and other societies in South Africa. He noted that for the Safwa, insofar as vital forces were believed to reside in ancestral spirits having a protective function, their interference into the affairs of the people could be either for good or bad.

---

1. Among those who give some attention to the consequences of colonial laws forbidding retaliation against those accused of witchcraft and against the practice of sorcery: Middleton and Winters (1963, p. 21); Fortune, Reo (1932, Appendix III. Administration and Society).

Kiernan (1982) reached much the same conclusion in his analysis of the part played by agency in the ascription of evil in South African societies. For him the folk model of evil, or better, the archetype of morality, was one of good *and* evil, in which ancestral spirits had constitutive roles to play as well as allocative, judicial roles. Although spirits of ancestors were essentially partisan, at times they stopped short of interceding in human affairs to prevent evil to preserve order and unity in society.

Kiernan must have been deeply moved by the dynamic, contrapuntal interpretations he culled from native accounts, for he told the reader that he "despaired" of solving the problem of evil. However, he was loath to abandon the task and proposed to substitute a sociological model of ethics for his purposes, using categories unrelated to theological and ethical distinctions.

An alternative way of thinking about evil is to accept moral ambiguity as one of its cardinal features, recognizing that its analysis necessarily moves into the vaguely charted areas of the implicit aspects of human affairs. This is because the durability of the special kinds of beliefs and activities associated with the effective imputation of evil necessarily rests on its ambiguity.

Evidence for the widespread association of evil and ambiguity is hardly deniable, given that it is typically described as emanating from occult or invisible power manifested by strange or unusual events, such as odd sounds at night, newly misplaced objects, and vague human statements of threat or looming danger. The Navaho, for example, never see witches; instead they see their "tracks" outside the hogan in the early light of day. Victims may suspect witchcraft or sorcery but in many cases seek out diviners or "clever" people to verify their fears and indicate suspects. However, diviners seldom named individuals, rather a type of person, such as "an old man" or a "woman with reddened eyes."

One of the more articulate statements on the matter of ambiguity was made by Fox (1967, p. 265) in his discussions of Cochiti witchcraft and its therapy. In this Pueblo society witches could appear as humans, animals, or even as fireballs. Suspicion was ubiquitous and practically everyone in the pueblo was suspected by someone at sometime of being a witch or practicing sorcery. To give Fox's general comment on the subject:

Witchcraft mythology is riddled with inconsistencies and it is often difficult to know whether an accused person is simply a "passive" witch, an active sorcerer, or an ordinary human in league with witches. Witchcraft accusations are rarely specific as to the nature of the witchcraft or the identification of victims. They simply say that he is a witch.

P. Turner (1970, p. 366) added a conclusive commentary on the multivocality in perceptions of witchcraft as he saw them expressed and acted out in accusations and counteraccusations among the Chontal of Mexico. In his words, "There must probably always be an element of ambiguity in witchcraft for it to be operative in any culture."

Much the same can be said more generally about the nature and agencies of evil in personifications other than in witchcraft, sorcery, and magic. As has already been noted, ancestral spirits given shape in beliefs in some African societies could be inconstant benefactors of the living, at times withholding their protection from evil events in the interests of social order and unity (Kiernan, 1982).

It is also true that spirits, gods, and goddesses of cosmic stature enshrined by human beings may be regarded as sources of both good and evil. In pantheons a kind of division of jurisdiction or specialization gave gods various areas of power for good and evil. Thus sky gods or creator gods generally were known to be guardians of law and order, while gods of the nether regions of the underworld often were portrayed as raging, destructive monsters. Yet creator gods also were known to exact punishment from errant mortals for their misdeeds and disturbances of order. Yahweh, the Old Testament god of the Hebrews, was so characterized, hence a source of evil as well as good. By the same token, underworld gods had softer moments when they favored rather than harassed people of the surface earth.

Evil as Ambivalent Power

All of this lends validity to Parkin's (1985, p. 13) assertion that the archetype of evil may be thought of profitably for comparative purposes as ambivalent power rather than simply the opposite of good. The empirical referents for this conception of evil are found in the tentative, uncertain way peoples of the world seek to account for misfortune and maleficence. While many of the peoples of Africa are wont to ascribe evils of their lives to human witchery and sorcery, not so for peoples in other parts of the world where there is a great variety of beliefs in spiritual, nonspiritual, and nonhuman agencies of evil; people relate these in complicated ways to God or even to an impersonal power.

It was when gods were anthropomorphized or personified as ethical, as images of goodness and power, that serious intellectual trouble began for human beings given to contemplation of cosmological aspects of good and evil. While the formal analysis of what came to be known as theodicies began with Kant and Liebnitz, the puzzle of how an all-powerful and loving god could tolerate vagaries of evil must have struck thinking victims of the world's misfortunes and human malice long before philosophers came on the scene.

My first encounter with what may be termed the poor man's theodicy occurred in graduate school when a fellow student working at the state capitol in Columbus, Ohio, idly confronted his Irish Catholic coworkers with a noontime puzzle, namely: "If God is all-powerful then he can make a rock so big he can't lift it." This did indeed create some mild consternation among his listeners, but a few days later, having consulted their parish priest, they came back with happy smiles and the reply that "God doesn't work in that way."

A God who works in mysterious ways may be part of the popular culture of good and evil of the American Christian and perhaps of the Jew as well. On the whole he is presumed to be hard at work on human problems, but at times he seems to be preoccupied or overworked. Or, to quote a quote attributed to Woody Allen, "The worst you can say of him is that he is an underachiever" (Griffin, 1991, frontispiece).

There is a grimmer aspect of theodicy recalled to us annually by the media and the rituals of the churches, that which Nietzsche (1956, p. 169) termed the "ghastly paradox of a crucified god." I refer to the implications of the words uttered by a drooping, lacerated, grievously wounded and dehydrated Christ who asks God why he has forsaken him—words spoken in the wind. This is brutal imagery not easily dismissed by catch phrases. It and the widespread calamities of deaths by war, incurable diseases, famine, and man's treatment of man continue to challenge philosophers and theologians to devise a rational solution to the puzzle of good, evil, and agency.

Evil as Process

I doubt very much whether the literature on theodicies can offer much to empirically based sociology. Nor can anthropology and sociology cast much useful light on the rarified concerns pursued by students of theodicies. Some might argue whimsically that functionalist theory in a very general sense, both in anthropology and sociology, provided something analogous to what I will here dub "sociodicies"—anthropology by celebrating witchcraft as a source of social conformity and social control; sociology by happily counting the ways deviances such as crime, prostitution, political corruption, and even poverty sustained the public weal. In retrospect functionalist theory, especially in sociology, carries the look of a dismal science, in some ways comparable to early economics.

In any case by the 1960s, anthropological studies of witchcraft as well as sociological studies of deviance had moved in the direction of process analysis, signalled by V. Turner's (1964) vigorous argument for a more dynamic interpretation of witchcraft. He spoke of the need for "process theory" involving a "becoming as well as being," and he insisted that accusations of witchcraft had to be examined in the context of social action. A necessary part of process, so conceived, was "considerable time depth," in short a historical dimension.

However, it was Nash (1967) who most closely approximated a process approach to witchcraft similar to the Meadian conception of symbolic interaction developed in deviance studies by sociologists in the 1960s and 1970s. Nash referred to a body of "cultural theory which leaves open the empirical definition of who is a witch" (p. 128). This aligned him, or perhaps the Tzetal Indians he studied, with the partisans of societal reaction theory (or those of labeling theory?) who held that deviance is subjectively problematical rather than objectively given. Note, too, that theologians in some cases recently have turned to the idea of "process theism" as a solution to the "problem of evil." This proposes God as a creator or as a principle of creativity rather than a king or entity (Griffin, 1991, p. 10f).

The ideas of social process and emergence phenomena have been around for a long time in sociology, however new they may have been to other fields. In fact, early American sociology at its University of Chicago stronghold essentially revolved around the study of social process or "the social processes." Unfortunately the process idea over time proliferated and was used in many different ways: historical and evolutionary change, group relationships leading to assimilation, socializing nonsocial or antisocial individuals into society, and the behavioral analysis of symbols in interpersonal interaction. Seen plainly, the process of interaction is not a theory so much as a condition of inquiry, calling for dynamic analysis of how one thing becomes something qualitatively different. The task in so doing requires attention to the importance of meaning in emergent phenomena. This is created in considerable part with the feedback from reactions that are social in nature; but from my perspective there also can be feedback from biological change as well as from the changes human beings make, wisely and unwisely, in their physical environment.

The Origins of Ideas about Evil

Despite my labored canvass of a sea of literature of the subject, I have met with no more than three discussions of ideas about evil sufficiently articulated to qualify as theories of their origins and historical development. Two of these, by Ricouer and Kavolis, recur to myths as data from which to infer how moral ideas of good, bad, and evil first arose among human beings and were transformed with time. The third, that of Nietzsche, draws from philosophy and biblical sources to sustain his often fervid statements on the subject. Just how to put these into logical order, given the ambiguous, protean nature of my subject matter, is by no means a simple task.

Ricoeur's (1967) theory reaches farthest back in time—to mythical chaos preceding the creation of human order. For its support he invokes a kind of primordial sociopsychological experience drawn from the Adamic myth as the first impulse to moral sensitivity and inner promptings of the human conscience. Accordingly, during the early or earliest period of human existence, social control grew out of feelings of defilement and ideas of guilt, presumably at a time when morality had a negative cast or a taboolike character emphasizing dangers to be avoided rather than pleasures to be sought. Objective fault became sin, which was conceived as offending spirits, demons, or a god. The evils they inflicted were dealt with by public confession and rituals. Thus among the early Jews, a priest made open confession in the name of the community, then laid hands on a goat to be sent into the wilderness.

As Judism became more institutionalized, a priestly office emerged through which a clerical elite preempted the definition of sin and evil along with the designation of sinners. Objectified evil that could be cast out was converted into moral evil, which was formalized and fixed by codes, thence internalized as guilt enjoining the individual's responsibility for his/her own actions. Orthodoxy and heresy became viable terms for deviant realities, determined by clerical sovereignty.

While Ricoeur's ideas may be a rough fit with the historical development of Hebraic morality, they scarcely serve as a universal model for the evolution of beliefs about evil in general. Reliance on unilinear interpretations of cultural change and reducing epochs of history to stages is perilous. In the present case one need only consult Goldenweiser's (1961, Part VI) updated version of the Golden Bough, crude though it is, to grasp some notion of the range of cultural differences in the riddance of evil through public rituals in very early societies. These reveal a wide variety of ends and pragmatic purposes served, certainly enough to sustain accepted skepticism about straight line evolution of human institutions.

Early Civilization and Evil

Kavolis (1984), a sociologist, undertook the historical comparative analysis of good and evil in part by reference to the content

of classical myths that he believed disclose universalistic understandings about the nature of evil, how they arise, the behavior
involved, and the social settings giving them substance. His most
readily understood statements compare the myths of Prometheus
and of Satan, both presumed to be prototypes of rebellion against
an established order. Prometheus steals fire and passes it on to
needy people without any expectation of praise or imposition
of restrictions on its recipients. In the course of defying his God,
Zeus, he also introduces comic relief by playing tricks with
bones on his superior. Prometheus is a humanitarian rebel with
a sense of humor. In contrast, now comes Satan, medieval vintage, who rebels out of resentment, his feelings fired by being
passed over at promotion time among the angels—obviously a
sorehead with little concern for the welfare of anyone but
himself.

From these myth models Kavolis concludes that the early
Greeks had a dialectical or processual attitude towards moral
issues that looked to the ultimate integration of recognized evil
with good. Just so, evil is transformed into good and challenges
it or encourages criticism of its claims. The opposite, the Satanic
model, reifies evil; its moral thrust in organized social control
is to validate the good and banish evil by dichotomizing them.
Evil is identified with deliberate disorder and willful contra-
vention of laws.

A Critical Note on Myths as Data

Whether myths represent universalistic moral ideas lurking
behind quaint symbolic productions in the cultures of early
societies is questionable at best. Hard-headed folklorists are
likely to be reserved on the matter if not openly critical. While
it is true that myths may justify cosmologies and morality,
nevertheless they are seldom well-defined and, recounted out
of context, they lose meaning, particularly since they tend to
be local in nature. Just how myths get used at different times
and places is not readily forecast, given the diversity and
perversity of the human condition.

I recall my one effort to record a text among Salish Indians
whose alcoholic habits I was studying years ago. Since I had only
half a pint of whiskey in my stores at the time, my Indian friends

urged me to give it to an older man, who downed it neat and
then proceeded to "tell us a story." This was about a man who
met a bear on the trail and was taken back to his den. There
the bear milled around, whuffled, farted, and complained to the
man about the tribulations of living with a she bear, but more
particularly about the difficulties of getting meat orders
delivered by boat from Eaton's Department store out of
Vancouver—and on it went in this vein. I can only best
characterize the storyteller as a stand-up comedian trying to
please his audience by adapting his materials to the situation.
One can conclude that myths are as myths are told and that
they reflect many influences, at least among the Tlahoose at
Squirrel Cove, British Columbia in the summer of 1952.

Nietzsche's Trilogy of Good, Bad, and Evil

While it overstates the case in retrospect to name Nietzsche a
sociologist, a modicum of premodern social psychology threads
through his trilogy of good, bad, and evil. Some of his concepts,
such as values and value judgments, are by no means archaic;
and there is more than a hint of present-day social construc-
tionism in his statement of the research question in the study
of morality—"Under what conditions did man construct the
value judgments of good and evil?" (Nietzsche, 1956, p. 157).
Moreover he anticipated Ricouer's searching interest in Hebraic
morality, but unlike him, was far more occupied with the collective and political aspects of moral evolution, knowable from
historical sources as well as from philology.

In his work *Human All Too Human*, Nietzsche first stated
his interpretation of the double evolution of good and evil
developed subsequently in *The Genealogy of Morals*. For him
the origins of morality lay in the elite or ruling classes—nobility
or aristocrats, primarily those in ancient Greece and Rome. Early
morality, said Nietzsche, grew out of pathos and distance,
coupled with the power of the upper classes to name things.
The early nobility saw disinctions between themselves and
commoners or plebeians as simple "good" and "bad." Good was
excellence in thought, spirit, and action; bad was no more than
the lack or absence of these qualities, etymologically derived

from terms like "simple" or "base." Added to these is the self-affirmation of the nobility as truthful, or more generally as representing the true reality, in conrast to that of lying plebeians.

The idea of evil as a drastic extrusion of bad, Nietzsche tells us, is traceable to the emergence of a priestly aristocracy that gave further meaning to "pure" and "impure" based on taboos and avoidance of foods, blood, and sex with unwashed plebeian women. In time these value oppositions were exacerbated and internalized, becoming a source of tension and conflict among men.

Here Nietzsche refers to the asceticism or antisensual metaphysics of the priestly caste as unwholesome and neurasthenic. Nevertheless he gives them credit due for setting man above animals by their capacity to deal with evil. Nietzsche saw in the distant past a priestly caste driven by abiding hatred (*resentiment*) due to their powerlessness, coupled with "brilliant politics of vengeance" against their oppressors, who replaced the good/bad distinction with a good/evil dichotomy. This was epitomized in the history of the Jews, who converted an aristocratic value system into slave ethics or a slave perspective on morality. This, furthered by the Christian movement, spread an inverted ideology of morality throughout the Western world, beknighting the poor, the deprived, and the lowly persons while condemning the affluent and the well-placed.

Nietzsche for all his brilliance was not an historian; his facts are allusive or thin at best, and lack provenience. It is true that the biblical Book of Revelations to which he refers starkly portrays evil at war with good, but it is not clear that Jews of the time were in agreement about the relationship of the two. Beyond this Nietzsche relies on a kind of reductionist psychology that ignores the plural nature of values and interests that are integrated into social movements.

It is doubtful if frustrated priests invented ideas about evil; more likely they exploited extant folk beliefs about magic, sorcery, and witchcraft for their religio-political purposes. However, I think that Nietzsche properly called attention to a distinction in the nature of moral ideas held by upper-class and lower-class members of society. In all likelihood this derived from the ability to read and write, which set upper classes apart, along with skills or arts associated with peripatetic teaching, mentorship, and patronage among those with affluence and power in early societies. Given this, it is likely that with more complete knowledge it could be shown that it was a morality of urban elites or of a "leisure class" that emerged from a popular culture of evil rather than the reverse, that ideas of good and evil subverted the morality of a literate noble class.

The interpretation gains from the penetrating work of Norman Cohn (1975), who has adumbrated a cultural history, going back to antiquity, of the belief in the existence of alien, troublesome groups given to evil ways—secret indulgence in cannibalistic feasts at which evil ones devoured children, gave over to sexual promiscuity, and committed incest.

With unfolding history the beliefs in the existence of such nefarious groups, possibly first directed at polytheistic peoples of the Near East by Jews, became later in the second century the basis for the persecution of Christians. An early instance of this is reported to have occurred in Lyons, France, in which after being subjected to mob violence along with their owners, the slaves of affluent Christians such as physicians and advocates, were tortured to give evidence of incestuous and cannibalistic orgies among their masters (Cohn, 1975, p. 4).

The essence of such beliefs, sometimes founded on misinterpretations of rituals such as the eucharist (eating the flesh of God symbolically), defined dissident religious minorities as antihuman and beyond the bounds of humanity, with the purpose of legitimating their persecution by those with power to do so. The universalistic nature of the underlying sociopsychological process at work is suggested by Cohn's observation that this was a pattern repeated many times in later centuries when orthodox Christians became the persecutors and other dissident or emarginalized groups, such as Jews, homosexuals, heretics, and witches, were victims (Cohn, 1975, p. 15).

It needs noting that patterns of persecution are complex and are not to be explained simply by reference to the content of beliefs of persecutors, nor by crude sociology of ingroup/outgroup divisions, nor by reductionist psychodynamic mechanisms of repression and projection. Rather patterns of persecution must be clothed and activated by the cultural specifics of historical or interactional convergences. In this connection Nietzsche's sharp separation of class moralities needs qualifying, since educated and highly placed persons have contributed to the substance of evil beliefs as well as those in the untutored lower classes.

Unfortunately history does not record sufficient information to meet explanatory requirements or test theories about the emergence of beliefs about evil. At most one may say that the universality of some such beliefs point to their possible inherent basis, or to ideas of evil as an ineluctable part of human experience. However, if history disappoints the questing scholar of evil it does not exhaust the perspectives at hand from which to view the subject. Among these is the experiential perspective, one which retains the conception of process but foreshortens it to focus on interpersonal and intergroup interaction.

2

Evil as Experience

At this point in what has grown into a considerable disquisition I will move beyond the troublesome efforts at characterizing evil in a substantive sense and beyond the exposition of theories as to its origins, causes, or functions. It will be more productive to clarify the kinds of human interaction and social situations that generate or sustain beliefs, language, action, and emotions associated with the attribution of evil and efforts at its social control. An immediate question comes to mind as to the importance of emotions and feelings relative to beliefs and language in the attribution and social control of evil.

Some of the most recent research and writing centered on evil comes from the work of what may be loosely termed a semantic school. I refer to *The Anthropology of Evil* edited by David Parkin (1985). The writers involved are generationally removed from theory and thought of the earlier anthropology of African witchcraft and sorcery and pointedly disregard consensualist interpretations of such phenomena. Instead they opt for the study of ideas and conceptions of evil, with a baseline assumption that explanations of evil encountered across cultures involves "essentially contested concepts." Parkin (1985, p. 23) summarizes as follows:

> More generally the main suggestions of this introduction are that evil refers to various ideas of perfection and excess seen as destructive: but these ideas are contestable concepts, which, when personified allow mankind to engage them in dialogue and reflect on the boundaries of humanity.

Unfortunately the semantic conception of evil, based largely on the study of language, downplays if it does not neglect the thrust of emotions from which evil as an attested experience derives. The semantic characterization comes out as a pallid one or, in the immediate context, as an overideated version of how a number of English scholars, identified with a culture given to minimizing display of emotion, see the matter.

A substantial literature argues for the reality of the experience of evil or to the necessity of so conceiving it. This presents the question of whether the testimony of individuals to the experience of evil, albeit ineffable and mystical, is prior to its symbolization or whether it can be treated as real apart from symbols by which it is articulated. Clearly there are qualified scholars who think so (Sanford, 1981, p. 41).

> Evil really is evil, or so, at least, we are compelled to experience it . . . unless this is kept in mind we are in danger of slipping into a sterile, intellectual solution to the problem that avoids the deep feeling response to evil which alone gives us an appreciation of its reality.

While the experience of evil cannot be identified exclusively with emotions any more than with ideas, much of the experience includes fear, anxiety, repulsion, and general sensual excitement. Hence, to perceive evil is not only to see with meaning but also to see with strong feelings. Nor are such perceptions confined to visual impressions for there can be a smell of evil as well as a look of evil, repulsive if not overpowering.

The Smell of Evil

Finer discussions of the experience of evil, because it reportedly involves such powerful affect, necessarily moves to psychological and physiological considerations in human perception. In fairness to Parkin, he does in his Introduction to *The Anthropology of Evil* posit a reality he calls descriptive evil (1985, p. 7). This has a semantic coating but nevertheless by reference to terms like "worthless," "crooked," "twisted," "unclean," "dirty," "black to rotten," and "bad" (as in decaying corpses of animals), descriptive evil does convey, at least in retrospect, its more sentient features.

Such terms need further elaboration to bring forth the felt primordial immediacy of evil, its ineffability, and pervasive power, irresistible and overwhelming. Ricoeur's (1967) idea of evil as defilement comes very close to the sensory basis for the perception of evil, especially taken to mean contamination and contagion linked with anxiety about physical death and the extinction of identity.

It is in the primitive and preindustrial rural locality groups in which the smell and sight of deathly decay is most commonly a part of daily experience that odors get linked with anxieties about death. The ascendancy of odor in the social elaboration of moral evil is for me best exampled by the Cheyenne word for murder, namely *putrid*. This connotation applied to the murder of one Cheyenne by another, all of whom were culturally conceived as brothers. The stench of murder fouled the sacred arrows of the tribe; it pervaded the camp and beyond, so that game avoided the area. The odor clung to objects used by the murderer such as dishes, for many years (Llewellyn and Hoebel, 1941, p. 12). In a comparable case, a band of Sioux, in which one member had murdered his cousin, acquired a reputation as an outlaw band, set apart from others by stigma that lasted through several generations (Crowdog and Erdoes, 1990, p. 197ff). A similar association of foul odor with evil was known as the *foetor-judaicus*, believed by people of the Middle Ages to be emitted by Jews as punishment for their murder of Christ (Tracktenberg, 1943, p. 48ff).

Visual Aspects of Evil

The visual premonitors of evil are less readily identifiable as the basis for its perception than those for odors. Why attributes like ugliness, misshapen, dirty, and sinistrality have evil implications is not immediately clear. At most it may be guessed that some sort of "disempathy" operates in the human perception process. Left-handedness as a case in point takes on evil (sinister) connotations in most cultures of the world, being seen as the opposite of "right" or "righteous" (Hertz, 1973). In medieval

Europe the bar sinister on a knight's shield signified his illegitimacy and possible source of conspiratorial trouble in societies in which status, land ownership, and wealth were hereditary.

Color, too, has associations with the perception of evil, probably resting on some inborn predisposition (Turner, 1969, p. 28).

> It seems likely that physiological factors underlying visual perceptions in all human beings have produced a high incidence in non-literate cultures of symbol systems that exploit chromatic differences of white, black and red.

Things dark, obscure, black, or red are connected with fear and anxiety in most cultures and often are associated with evil (Russell, 1977, p. 64; Parsons, 1927; Willis, 1985, p. 216). Fear of the dark or total blackness stems from spatial disorientation and possible painful experiences as well as from cultural transmission. This fear may even have a genetic source in the evolutionary persistence of such fears. Here one can speculate with some assurance that early man or his progenitors before the discovery of fire had well-justified fears of nighttime predators, especially leopards, saber-tooth tigers, and hyenas, much as do present day primates sleeping in trees at night.[1]

Fears described here conceivably were bequeathed to modern man, then reinforced by awareness that many violent crimes, such as burglary, robbery, arson, and assault, are committed under the cover of darkness. So Aubert (1982, ch. 2) tells us, "Night is a time for surreptitious activities . . . but nighttime

---

1. Coss has found large and significant directional difference in the sources of nighttime fears of small children, with girls' fears coming from below and boys' fears coming horizontally. This is consistent with observed behavior of primates among whom females and their young sleep high in trees, while dominant males sleep in the lower branches. See Coss, Richard G., Spatial Location of Children's Nighttime Fears. *Report.* Nov. 20, 1991. University of California at Davis.

Support evidence that early proto humans were subject to predation in trees by carnivores comes from South African archeological research. Brain, C. K. 1970. *New Finds at Swartkans Australopithecine Site.* Nature (Lond.) 225, 1112–1119.

is even more massively defined as a time for evil and crime." Likewise, night is a time for sleep, when human neurophysiology changes completely and "dream reality prevails that is unrelated to action" (Bushnell, 1869).

The Evil Eye

The widespread belief in the existence of the evil eye suggests an association of some sort between eye contact and evil. Staring—even pictures of eyes—in some forms and contexts activate fear, avoidance, and aggressive reactions in both man and beast, so much so that eye contacts can be regarded as universal signals. Although regulated by norms, gaze behavior does not vary much between cultures, so that looking too much or too little have similar meanings (Argyle and Cook, 1976, chs. 7, 8).

It is more than speculation that persons impute or encode evil from visual and other associated behavior cues arising in social interaction. The hospitable reception sociologists and others give to Max Weber's (1958) conception of charisma supports the general idea that a distinctive kind of interpersonal attraction does exist between persons who have no objective grounds for explaining it. Most references to charisma phrase it as positive attraction, but its opposite, negative charisma, has been proposed by several writers, anthropological as well as sociological, to designate attraction between enemies or specifically between witches and their victims in the sense that, "persons are disvalued but have unusual influence over others" (Turner, P., 1970; Aberle, D., 1966; Katz J., 1972).

Just what the neurological or neuropsychological basis is for the perception of evil or the concomitant linkages between the strong feelings involved and human biology are, has not been studied extensively.[2] However, what can be said with confidence is that human beings do have mystical, meaning ineffable, experiences. We need not simply rely on William James' (1985)

---

2. Mary Douglas stated that witchcraft themes recognized in cultures "across the globe" while highly variable "have a biopsychic basis to exploit." See her *Confessions and Accusations*, 1970, London, Tavistock, Introduction, xxvi.

early insistence on their reality, based on anecdotal evidence, to make the point (Greeley & McReady, 1974). It is well known that subcortical integrations of the human nervous system do occur, that subliminal stimulation and response are empirically established facts, and that perception can be affected by changes in the awareness of feedback signals that monitor human feeling and action: auditory, visual, kinesthetic, tactile, and olfactory. The simplest illustration is that of the blind person who learns to respond to cues ignored by those with sight such as traffic sounds or cross movements of air at junction points of corridors. George H. Mead (1956) referred to this aspect of learning as immediate experience in contrast to the fragmented awareness that is socially or culturally learned. This distinction has been elaborated in an article by Boyle (1985) on the "Dark Side of Mead," which explores a neuropsychological explanation for altered perception, or the enlargement of its span to include that which is ordinarily regarded as mystical.

Somehow, someway, the changes in awareness and altered sensory states that go with the perception of evil get coupled with fear; or perhaps it is better to say that fear does the coupling, an idea phrased by the adage "fear has a thousand eyes." The fear in question is most fittingly described as terror, whose root is *tres*, meaning to tremble. This speaks of exacerbated anxiety, verging to panic, set apart from terror engendered by natural disasters, by ambiguity as to its source, and by emotions of loathing, disgust, and abhorrence. The statement of a sixteenth-century writer, Bodin (1580, p. 18), also a presiding judge at witchcraft trials during this time, spoke to the intensity of feeling towards defendants:

> the very concept of witch stems from a deep-seated terror induced by a threat and a desire to ferret out the cause of the menace and violently eradicate it so as to re-establish peace and security.

Another writer emphasizes the sense of immediacy and urgency in the motivations of human beings leading them to personify evil and put an end to it (Graubard, 1984):

Man's response to invasion, illness or any other menace is that something must be done, something can be done. This response serves the goal of self preservation. His gut response is that someone is causing the mischief and that evil somebody must be stopped.

Evil as Negative Emotions

There is much to indicate that, beginning with Evans-Pritchard's (1937) work, a number of early anthropologists doing field studies of witchcraft and sorcery, as well as the later semanticist school more generally concerned with evil, neglected the singular emotional nature of their subject matter. In any case Evans-Pritchard's statement about the easy accommodation of community members to the presence of suspected witches and their lack of preoccupation with witchcraft in everyday existence struck inconsistent notes with the emphasis he put on the associated malice and hatred. This slighting of psychological factors in the analysis of Azande witchcraft was noted in the following commentary (Kennedy, 1967, p. 218):

> Evans-Pritchard underplays the emotional turbulence and irrational side of these practices. For example, in spite of the fact that most deaths and almost all other misfortunes are attributed to witches and the behavior is (from his own description) full of hostility and strife he lays great stress on the fact that witchcraft as perceived by the Azande is an everyday concern which inspires no fear, mystery or dread.

It may be more accurate to say that Evans-Pritchard's fine-honed reporting reflected ambiguities on the issue that remained unresolved in his presentation. Thus for example, the author says that accusations of witchcraft were situational and that hostile feelings they aroused were subsequently dissipated. Yet he also says that some persons were so frequently accused that they acquired reputations as witches (p. 112). He distinguished the "position of the witch" yet added that the witch "lives like an ordinary citizen" and that "some of his best friends were witches." Evans-Pritchard then added that, "No one would risk living near an old man witch in the settlement," and notes that there "were violent outbreaks against him" (p. 15).

There are a number of possible reasons why Evans-Pritchard and the first ethnographers of African witchcraft had difficulty in fitting emotions and sentiments into their interpretations of their findings. First was their concern with primitive mentality and the apparent need to find a rational explanation for that which on the surface struck them as irrational. Evans-Pritchard recognized that he confronted subject matter that was "difficult for Europeans to understand," and that it was so foreign that it "is hard to appreciate its reality" (p. 540). Seligman echoed this misgiving in his foreward to Evans-Pritchard's book on the Azande (p. xvi).

Confronted by the seemingly unassailable convictions of their native informants that witches murdered people, Evans-Pritchard and ethnographers who followed with like interests understandably paid more attention to beliefs than they did to emotions in their interpretations of data. No theoretical scheme emerged from their work that effectively incorporated these two aspects of their subject matter.

A second problem for the field researchers in question was their self-imposed quest for some kind of consistency or coherence in the native explanations of their beliefs and the associated behavior. Evans-Pritchard started his work by looking for evidence of "an ideological system in witchcraft beliefs and their social expression." Others in the field drew from functionalist theories current among English anthropologists at midcentury or they developed perspectives influenced by French structuralism psychology and writings of Radcliffe Brown (1952).

In the conclusions of his study of the Azande, Evans-Pritchard was compelled to admit that the author creates a conceptual system of beliefs about witchcraft, but actually they are not indivisible ideational structures. In real life they do not function as a whole but in bits. The native in one situation "utilizes" what in the beliefs are convenient to him and pays no attention to other elements he might use in different situations.[3] Evans-Pritchard's faithful reporting carefully avoided reifying the concept of a system and left room in his thinking for the Azande as persons who exercised choices (p. 546) and not merely those who "express" social factors.

Evans-Pritchard, while critical of the concept of a system, did not reconcile his own conflicting observations about the emotional concomitants of witchcraft. Other anthropologists presumably influenced by views such as Radcliffe Brown's (1952, p. 282) that positive and negative rites (good and evil) exist and persist as part of a mechanism for preserving social order, in effect created a kind of "sociodicy" or a justification for social order analogous to the theodicies of theologians who rationalized God's justice. From this view, the castigation, expulsion, and killing of witches had socially desirable functions, such as providing common explanations for misfortunes, excuses for personal failures, increasing lineage solidarity, and lineage splitting which redistributed population (Gray, 1963). Thus good comes from evil.

Such interpretations tell comparatively little about the feelings and emotional reactions of community members to witchcraft, particularly with respect to their influence on thought and choices of action. In no small degree this follows from the imposed vocabulary of concepts such as norms, rules, structure, social codes, archetypes, conformity, nonconformity, and ideology often used in functional analysis.

A feasible way to avoid misconstruing or "sociologizing" the native perspective on witchcraft is to distinguish between normative ideas and existential ideas, similar to G. H. Mead's (1956) fragmented awareness versus immediate experience. It is doubtful whether morality as it is known in technologically developed societies of the West is adequate as a basis for understanding the conflict and social control in tribal societies.

Morality in such simple, isolated societies generally is realized in action; it tends to be implicit and recognized in

---

3. Much the same conclusion was reached by Pitt-Rivers (1964) in his study of witchcraft beliefs in a Mexican village: "In a word, the conceptual system becomes a whole 'systematic' only in the context of action as a means of integrating events with the history of the community."

retrospect, as rationalizations, usually in terms of "what should have been" (Read, K.E., 1987). Self and role are not separated. A good deal of research goes to the prime importance given by many tribal or isolated village peoples to feelings of amity, civility, and affective reciprocity for maintaining harmony within the community (Arensberg, 1917; Ito, 1987; Briggs, 1970). A much better term than norms or rules to describe such desiderata is *correct sentiments*, the bulk of which are oriented to heightened sensitivity towards others as sentient human beings.

Gluckman (1965, p. 237) stated his belief that an obligation bound tribal members to a duty not to harm one another, reflecting a legalistic view of amity and civility and extending it to feelings as well as actions. A later (1972, p. 41) statement gave his view a strong moral basis:

> The ambivalence in close personal relationships which dominate in tribal society leads to an exaggerated emphasis on the importance of others as part of their responsibility to their fellows, feeling towards these fellows correct sentiment . . . a premium is set on such people feeling as well as acting correctly towards one another.

However, Moore (1972, p. 63) challenged this view on grounds that Gluckman's "duty not to harm" when examined more closely did not mesh well with the occurrence of violence and the use of coercion in simple societies. Sounding very much like Oliver Wendell Holmes, she held that while there is a recognized liability for harm it translates into no more than a "duty to pay," a rule not infrequently needing enforcement.

Dichotomizing tribal and modern societies sometimes carries a kind of nostalgic idealization of the former that ignores the possibility that human concern for others does not enlighten social interaction in all such societies. Gillen (1934) discussed attitudes of Barama River Caribs on the issue:

> On the secular side, law and justice are highly personal. Only in cases . . . in which the individual by the multiplicity and pertinacity of his offenses makes himself

a public nuisance do members of the group take united action against him, and in such cases it appears that group action is taken as a result of the sum of individual grievances rather than from a conscious sociological consideration for the welfare of the group as an entity . . . little attention is paid to abstract ideals of right and wrong. A Carib is only mildly interested in offenses suffered by other individuals.

What Gillen does not say and Gluckman does is that interpersonal hostilities can and do disrupt the working of productive and political units in low-energy societies as well as their more intimate groupings. Colson (1953) documented the point convincingly with data on Tonga people that showed how whole families were sundered by the slowness with which one epinymic group responded to demands of another in the event a recognized troublemaker among the former had committed an outgroup murder.

So much for the "heightened sensitivity" of persons in tribal societies to the feelings of others as a specific determinant of action. In some cases such sensitivity led to immediate violence, as among those African peoples who were quick to respond to insults, noted by Moore (1965, p. 64f). In other societies, such as the Samoans, it produces brooding, indwelling anger, after days or weeks erupting over trifling incidents into murderous rage and machete carnage (Lemert, 1972, p. 230; Marsack, 1959). The Caribs apparently could care less about interpersonal sensitivity.

Two Themes of Social Control

The treatments of beliefs and emotions in anthropological studies of witchcraft and sorcery produced two disjunctive themes of social control. In one, witchcraft beliefs are featured as a source for the symbolic social control of deviance; the other has to do with the disruptive emotions arising in interpersonal conflict and the part played by the community in such conflicts. Its concern is less that of attempted control of witchcraft *per se* than with its emotional antecedents in social interaction.

The first theme of social control rests directly on the notion that beliefs in witchcraft acted as a means of social control that produced compliance with cultural norms. The idea that beliefs control behavior, by no means new, was first offered by E. A. Ross in 1901 in his book on *Social Control*, which had a theoretical kinship with early group mind theories of French social psychology. The theme was furthered by the influence of Durkheim's conception that collective moral representations are reaffirmed by the rituals of punishment of criminals. The unanimity of early African ethnographers of witchcraft and sorcery on the subject is herewith noted (La Fontaine, 1963, p. 217):

> It has become a truism that witchcraft beliefs act as a form of social control in discouraging behavior that is socially unacceptable.

According to this view, control in the African context derived from the portrayal of the witch as a symbol of all that is bad and to be avoided. In sum the African witch was believed to commit a whole gamut of deviance and indecencies: sodomy, homosexuality, incest, disinterring and feasting on corpses, consuming toads and rats, running about naked, filthiness, defecating in fields and public places and girls' sleeping areas, urinating in milking receptacles, poisoning others, seducing young girls, hanging upside down, eating salt when thirsty, plus consorting with leopards and riding hyenas.

Dramatization of Evil

The process through which, according to ethnographers of the day, individuals were turned away from such evil ways was dramatization (Marwick, 1967 p. 124):

> It is widely held that beliefs in witchcraft—and the same would hold for sorcery—are an effective means of dramatizing social norms in that they provide in the person of a mystical evil-doer a symbol of all that is held to be anti-social and illegitimate.

Dramatization and personification by means of texts, songs, and plays have long been regarded as means of moral indoctrination; but the stereotypes of the African witch seem more like bestialization than personification. I fail to see or comprehend why or how such things as feasting on corpses, rats, and toads, hanging upside down, and consuming salt to slake one's thirst, or consorting with leopards and riding hyenas has any plausible connection with moral indoctrination. This despite one ingenious contention that the African witch's behavior was a reverse or mirror image of moral goodness necessary to personify evil (Winter, 1963, p. 292; Middleton, 1954).

The witch pictured in African studies is viewed as inhuman rather than human, an alien, an outsider, or as one beyond redemption or control, whose behavior was gross, capricious and unpredictable—hardly a candidate for a role in a drama in which moral ideas compete with one another and lead to some ultimate resolution. At most the hideous depiction of the witch provided a means of justifying the extreme measures taken to rid groups or communities of those typified as enemy aliens (Znaniecki, 1963; 347).

Actually there is not very much in the African witchcraft literature to document the idea that norms were effectively dramatized in the manner, for example, in which Durkheim characterized the punishment of criminals as affirmation of collective morality. Nor is there much written on the subject comparable to the pomp and pageantry of law demonstrated in criminal trials of eighteenth-century England.

Dramatistic analysis in the style of Erving Goffman (1967) is only indirectly suggested by the witchery ethnographers. In any case such analysis is possible only when there is agreement on the goals and clarity of rules of the human actions being studied (Messinger, 1962). The uncertainty surrounding accusations of witchcraft and their outcomes make it unlikely that they could have been viewed as forms of dramaturgy with any degree of success.

Containing Conflict

What has to be said points to a second theme of social control in witchcraft and sorcery materials of Africa, namely that accusations of such evil work arose out of interpersonal conflict rather than deviance from definable community norms. The dominant issue shifts from whether someone committed immoral acts such as incest or homosexuality to the resolution of personal conflicts and restoration of peace and harmony within the community. La Fontaine (1963, p. 219) put it in this way in her interpretation of witchcraft among the Bugisu:

> The 'ideology' of witchcraft accepts the fact of conflict and explains it in terms of dyadic relationships . . . an accusation of witchcraft places responsibility on both the accused and the accuser . . . to maintain amity by right behavior.

While this scholar invoked the dramaturgic metaphor current at the time, nevertheless she put emotions rather than normative behavior at the center of her thought when she states (p. 214):

> witchcraft accusations, consultations with diviners and the ritual of counter magic dramatize the destructive forces of interpersonal strife. . . .

For further emphasis on the crucial place of affect in analysis, La Fontaine refers to the "part played by the witch in the archetype of evil," in which the "hideousness of the witch's act further condemns the emotions with which he regards others . . . ."

Who Gets Accused

The divergence between the two themes of social control was more than matched by the diverse characterizations of persons in Africa and mid-American villages most likely to be accused of witchcraft and sorcery. These included identifiable physical or behavioral characteristics, such as dirty, ugly, deformed, or with unkempt appearances. In other cases deviant acts rather than appearance served to mark persons said to be inclined to witchcraft and sorcery, such as incest and homosexuality. Status

indicators, such as age, sex, socioeconomic position, or membership in a stigmatized lineage, also appeared as distinguishing
marks of those suspected of evil machinations against others.
Different accounts listed status as "outsiders," including out-
married wives, migratory workers, miners, local business men,
and sometimes simply "neighbors," as those likely to be targets
of suspicion of witchcraft and sorcery in African societies.

Historical and theological literature is rich with references
and images of women as evil and sources of pollution or temptation. The recent burgeoning historical studies of witchcraft during
the fifteenth and sixteenth centuries in Europe, especially in
English and Scotch villages of the period, singled out older
women, often widows of limited economic means, as those apt
to attract the suspicions of others. Likewise women predominated
as witches in some African societies (La Viu, 1963, p. 229f). Yet
the Navaho Indians most often directed their suspicions of
witchery towards older, affluent men, some of whom held important positions as ritual singers (Kluckhohn, 1944, pp. 111, 251).

The interest in the demographic features of witch suspects
in African studies undoubtedly came from efforts to demonstrate
that loci in social structure of the community best explained
sources of interpersonal conflicts, which in turn generated
witchcraft accusations. The demography of those accused jibed
with the structuralist premises favored by anthropologists then
at work in the African field, but was less applicable to Kluckhohn's findings for the Navaho.

Unfortunately attempts at characterizing those most likely
to be accused of witchcraft in both African and aboriginal
American populations did not clearly distinguish between
witches and sorcerers, or ordinary persons in league with
sorcerers. The fact that community members believed that
shamans, curers, and medicine men sometimes used their
powers for their own purposes further obscures the picture.
Moreover, informants asserted that good people were not always
what they seemed to be, with implications that hate and envy
motivating witchcraft and sorcery were endemic among human
beings. This recalls Fox's (1967) commentary on witchcraft
among the Pueblo peoples, namely that practically everyone was
suspected at some time or another (infra, 21).

In summary, one may tentatively conclude that in relatively stable tribal societies witchcraft accusations more frequently identified a distinctive type or class of people. However, not so necessarily in societies fraught with intrusive socioeconomic changes and pervaded by interpersonal tensions. Many if not most African societies in the early and midcentury had come under colonial powers bringing disruptive political and legal changes. A number of ethnographers of the period concluded that witchcraft and sorcery fears grew apace under these conditions (La Fontaine, 1963).

Best evidence on this matter lies in Kluckhohn's (1944, p. 144ff) findings that subjugation of the Navahos by the U.S. government made witchcraft a substitute for war, and that "white pressure" from the Indian Service programs and the outlawing of witchcraft trials led to the resurgence of witchcraft practices. Exceptions have been noted, namely that witchcraft accusations did not increase in some societies subjected to urban influences (Douglas, 1970; Wilson, 1945; Mitchell, 1965). Closer study might have shown that urban influences maintained or increased the potential for witchcraft accusations but interfered with the process of accusation and thus dissipated the basis for their community support.

Parenthetical with these observations it must be noted that all societies produce a range of personalities, some of whom by reason of special biological or social influences, or both, may be deemed antisocial by others. This term and its synonyms suggest that native informants typified certain persons as witchcraft suspects based not only on their overt actions but also on a socially undesirable attitude. A term for this, given currency in deviance sociology, is that of *demeanor*, which refers to deviant behavior coupled with a defiant manner or remorseless attitude.

Persons so typed tend to be solitary, surly, arrogant, uncooperative, self-centered, contumacious, or mean. Some when clinically diagnosed in our society may be called sociopaths or psychopaths. Buxton (1963, p. 104f) refers to such persons among the Mandari of the Southern Sudan: "bad people were those who talk anyhow." Such people were very outspoken or made obscure references to people's appearances and activities, or they "repeat or use people's proper names along with strong and biting speech." Parsons (1927) stated that "a reckless attitude towards others and not caring what you say" was one indication of witchhood to Zuni Indians.

Paiute Indians (Whiting, 1950) indicated the likely witch suspect as: "anyone who frequently loses his temper, who criticizes others in their presence, who does not look others straight in the eyes, and is said to be mean." This plausibly suggests that the interaction of such persons with others had a special self-reinforcing quality that reflected their unenviable status.[4]

Goffman (1967) described implicit "rules" of tact in interpersonal interaction, whose disregard by persons of the sort depicted in the above paragraph could "cause trouble":

> Tact in facework . . . relies . . . on a tacit agreement to do business through a language of innuendo, ambiguities, carefully worded jokes, and so on. . . . The rule regarding this unofficial kind of communication is that the sender ought not to act as if he conveyed the message he hinted at . . . it is no wonder trouble is caused by persons who cannot be relied upon to play the face-saving game.

In a statement more directly bearing on issues of emotionality Goffman adds a further "must" to his rule of civility (p. 108):

> The person must restrain his emotional involvement so as not to present an image of a person with no self-control or dignity, who does not rise above his feelings.

---

4. So-called "witch finders" apparently used similar identifying characteristics in selecting persons for "cleansing" action: . . . their mystical attitudes are readily credited to unpopular people of dour or difficult temperaments, bad mixers in the American sense, bad sharers, or persons who seem to be winning unusual success at other peoples' expense (Richards, Audrey, *A Modern Movement of Witchfinders: Africa*, viii (1935), 448–61).

3

Some Realities of Social Control

One of the reasons why formal means fall short in dealing with socially disruptive emotions inheres in the intimate, idiosyncratic, and often ambiguous nature of interpersonal interaction for whose control rule and remedy are difficult to devise. To illustrate the point, one can ironically imagine a judge in a court of law ordering a miscreant to follow Goffman's facework "rule" of interaction and to be tactful in dealing with others on the pain of a fine or a jail term. Much the same can be said of the methods of present-day police, who daily encounter or experience the "evil" people do to one another. Police cynicism about the reach of law into interpersonal problems shows clearly in their reluctance to make arrests on complaints against lovers, mates, relatives, or close friends (Black, 1983).

Intimate interpersonal interaction by definition means that continuous, often idiosyncratic evaluation occurs between the individuals involved; and it is for this reason that values rather than rules commend themselves as the better basis for understanding the kinds of deviance identified as evil. Kluckhohn (1944), while acknowledging the normative aspects of witchcraft, nevertheless emphasized value clusters such as familism necessary to understand hosility towards certain witchcraft suspects. Even more explicitly, Selby's study (1974) indicated that the disregard for certain cultural values, those of trust, respect and humility, was crucial for stirring suspicions of witchcraft among the Zapotec.

The social control of human sentiments in general or of individuals regarded as "antisocial," such as the "enfant terrible," the "acting-out adolescent," the "freeloader," the "boor," the "smart ass," the "bully," or the "troublemaker" often, if not typically, is a difficult and sometimes impossible task. In the same vein, intervention in personality conflicts, or in those between husbands and wives, is often fruitless, counterproductive, or even dangerous.

Years ago Linton (1936, pp. 220ff.) properly stated that the high visibility of everyday life in the locality group and the intimate knowledge people had of one another in such groups made premeditated offenses like theft rare. However, unpremeditated deviance like sexual infidelity and violence at best could only be influenced by preventive controls, such as gossip, or at times by actual encouragement of interpersonal hostility to bring it to a head and limit its destructiveness.

Some societies, like the Eskimo, sought to contain violence through semi-institutionalized means, such as wrestling contests or so-called juridical drum fests (Hoebel, 1968). Even these were optional and they did not always prevent assaults and murders.

The Arusha people of what was Northern Tanganyika strongly disapproved of self-help as social control and accordingly organized conclaves and assemblies for the negotiation of disputes between individuals, but they remained ambivalent about the use of coercion for their settlement. Supernatural controls such as ritual peace oaths also were employed. Nevertheless, private curses and witchcraft persisted among these people, the latter clearly indicated by the periodic antiwitchcraft drives by the women in the villages (Gulliver, 1963, p. 289).

Given variation in cultural values and the presence or absence of dispute settlement procedures in different societies, one is likely to agree with ethnographers who generally have emphasized that the evils of witchcraft and sorcery arose in areas of social interaction that could not be subjected to formal social control. Evans-Pritchard (1937) spoke of these as actions "beyond the reach of criminal and civil law." Buxton (1963, p. 107) put the problem even more persuasively:

. . . modern fieldwork research has shown that in many societies the "witch" is largely a symbolic personality standing for moral feelings which are condemned but which cannot be dealt with by direct punitive sanctions.

Informal Controls—Gossip

Apart from the semiformalized techniques of social control alluded to here, such as among the Eskimo, may be found verbal exhortations and appeals to adhere to correct emotions as means of defusing potential trouble in small isolated communities. However, these may be risky and alienate those who try this kind of peacemaking. An alternative is gossip, which provides an indirect sanction when the risk of more direct action is great or when no other sanctions are at hand. Gossip preserves the appearance of amity within a community and can, among other things, be a means of discrediting other persons (Paine, 1967, p. 278; Herskovitz, 1937). Over-used, it may mark the person as a gossip monger, discrediting the discrediter.

Given the often noted sensitivity of African tribal people to being thought a witch, one might have expected gossip to have figured more significantly in discussions of their efforts to control witchery and sorcery. However, this was not the case.

In contrast to the sparse references to gossip in African societies, Kluckhohn's (1944) study of the Navaho includes a number of informative accounts of witchcraft gossip (pp. 96, 98, 111, 117, 119, 123). This he distinguishes from accusations by reference to the "threat of accusation," or to "be spoken of as a witch." Moreover Kluckhohn credits a great deal of influence to witchcraft gossip in serving individual purposes as well as reducing intragroup tensions. It may be that the special turbulent history of the Navaho, at one juncture allegedly counting the execution of "more than forty witches" (pp. 172ff.), gave extra force to witchcraft gossip and the threat of accusations.

Selby (1974), who wrote with the idiom of modern deviance theory in mind, spoke of the "social process of gossip" as the means for identifying and labelling witches among the Zapotec, a process he explicated by enumerating the different frequencies with which informants designated another person as a witch, plus the frequencies of their overlap. Zapotec villagers described witchcraft gossip as "being different" from other gossip in that they remembered it for a long time (pp. 118ff.). This fact about witchcraft gossip also was noted by Kluckhohn (p. 241, footnote 80).

The Sociology of Accusation

What has been called the sociology of accusation has largely centered on attributes of persons likely to be accused of witchcraft or sorcery and their implications for the structural basis of their "evil" actions. A more dynamic perspective shifts attention away from structure to the process by which this takes place—to be understood as a form of extended case analysis which speaks of an outcome rather than a definitive conclusion of witchcraft or sorcery episodes. Ordinarily the process starts with individuals who confront untoward events, such as a personal misfortune or a quarrel with another person. The unfortunate event gives rise to brooding or mind searching by the potential accuser who develops some idea of who might be the persecutor. At this point the individual may talk with others or gossip about the problem. Generally this leads to consulting a diviner, a curer, a witch smeller, a magician, witch doctor, the cunning man, or wise person. This part of the process is substantiated by similarities between witchcraft accusations in African tribal societies and those in English villages in Sussex county in the fifteenth and sixteenth centuries, also having something in common with the analysis of the "micropolitics of trouble" in modern society described by Emerson and Messinger (1977).

In some instances the "victim" of suspected witchery consulted several diviners, shopped around in a sense, to find one whose suspicions coincided with his/her own. Beyond such assistance a diviner might help the client by making counter-magic against the suspected witch, but more often a recognized sorcerer was sought out for the purpose, sometimes from afar. In some areas these sorcery doers resembled "hired guns" of the Old West and they took satisfaction from the awe or fear they inspired. All of this suggests some kind of universal tendency for persons faced with pressing and inexplicable events to turn to others for some kind of testing and reassurance as to the reality of their experience as well as for social support and succor.

The accusatory process among the Azande was greatly individualized since they consulted with various kinds of oracles to objectify fears of witches, the poison chicken oracles being prominent among them.[1] A seance conducted by a number of witch doctors served a similar purpose, but in much more elaborate form. Evans-Pritchard (1937) spent many pages on detailed description of these, but he failed to relate them in any significant way to community opinion other than to note in a few short paragraphs that the witch doctor seance helped to gain support and recognition . . . and publicity for the master of the homestead who opened his house (p. 164) for seances.

This omission prompted E. P. Peters (1967) to reinterpret Evans-Pritchard's data with a showing that oracles did not give verdicts on witches but rather influenced the community of Azande persons who used them. This applied especially to the seance of the witch doctors, for these specialists skillfully detected public suspicions and artfully molded them into a consensus among their audiences. They gauged the support available in the community for the condemnation of a resident with faulted social relationships falling outside of ordinary jural relationships.

Trials and Formal Control

The place of trials and formal procedure in the social process leading to action against a suspected witch or sorcerer in tribal society remains vague since ethnographic accounts at best are cursory on the matter. A general impression is that they took the form of hearings, or community inquests, or as occasions for administering ordeals rather than as trials in the manner of fifteenth and sixteenth century European witchcraft trials. Van Valkenburg (1937) claimed that the Navaho conceived witchcraft as a crime; but the lack of a fixed procedure for introducing evidence, for arguments, and for making judgments makes this claim tenuous. Navaho "trials" followed when a

---

1. The Azande when perturbed about personal problems and possible witchcraft administered poison to chickens along with queries as to whence came the evil influences. If the fowl died it meant one kind of answer; if it lived it meant another. Usually when the fowl died it confirmed the suspicion held by the person giving the poison, i.e., that a certain person, or a member of a certain household was directing witchcraft at him or his household (Evans-Pritchard, 1937, pp. 304ff.).

group of tribesmen, convinced by one individual's suspicion of another, or by divination, called a meeting to which the suspect was brought, led by a rope. His captors urged him to confess, and if not, tied him down without food, water, or bladder relief until he did. Navahos believed that confession by the "witch" could stay the progress of a victim's illness. Failure to confess in four days meant death from a mass attack by clubs and axes.

In other instances, when feelings ran very high, the aggrieved victim simply shot the "offender" or he and his partisans carried out the execution without invoking a trial. Those taking less drastic action might allow the culprit to escape on condition that he leave the area. The use of clubs by a diverse group to dispatch a suspected witch may have had a connection with such precipitous action in that identification of the person striking the fatal blow was made difficult as well as complicating any demands for compensation by relatives of the wasted witch.

The interests and participation of the community in validating such executions was detailed in Nash's (supra, 24) account of the killing of a suspected witch among the Tzeltal, which much better illustrates community reaction than does Kluckhohn's report. Nash generalizes that a society "must have some social machinery" to differentiate between a murder and the elimination of a witch by an aggressor who acts in the name of the community. Put somewhat differently one may say that when communities seek to avoid the risk of escalated conflict, its members are likely to validate such actions by public hearings.

Among the Tzeltal a person stressed by witchcraft suspicions not only used a diviner to identify the suspect but also, according to belief, had him negotiate by sending his "narwale," or animal spirit, to talk with the witch's narwale. If this eased the victim's sore plight then nothing more was done. But if it worsened—his sick child died, for example—he brooded further and nursed his anger until he, along with kinsmen and friends, killed the witch from ambush. A shotgun blast did the deed, or they kicked the person relentlessly or hacked him with machetes until he was dead.

Subsequently the instigator of the slaying appeared before local officials in a community building where a "judge" conducted a hearing. Relatives, neighbors, and others gave testimony, in an instant case that the man was drunkard, irresponsible, a novice curer who was overly aggressive and "did not properly abide by age respect rules in social interaction." Both wife and kinsmen in effect washed their hands of the affair and disowned the dead man. The presider concluded that the slayer was an honorable man, who acted as an executioner, not a murderer. Later when Mexican police arrived to invesigate, they received all of the details of the man's death but no word of suspects whatsoever from the villagers.

Goody (1970) described a somewhat more extensive procedure for the social control of female witches in the African state of Gonja, part of Ghana. Its place as part of a federation generated a form of administrative justice organized around the responsibility of chiefs to protect their tribal members from witchcraft aggression, primarily by women. The male chiefs of the compounds, who allegedly had powers of seeing and identifying the evil female witches, reported their discoveries to the village chief. The latter, also believed to have "benign" witch powers, ordered certain rituals to be performed to identify publicly and warn the witch in question. If this failed its purpose, the chief ordered her to drink water from a shrine that, when drunk, supposedly induced death from merely contemplating any further evildoing. Otherwise he commanded her to leave the area.

If all of these measures met with opposition from the witch, the village chief took her to a divisional chief who heard the case in a council hall in the presence of all concerned, both accusers and kin of the accused. In pre-European times if the chief found the accused guilty, an executioner beheaded her, or impaled her on a stake, or crowned her with a red hot cooking pot, or burned her alive in an earthen pit. Afterwards the woman's property was divided between the executioner and the chief.

The inordinate cruelty of all of these forms of execution provides one possible instance in African societies of the dramatization of evil comparable to public executions that distinguished pre-nineteenth-century English criminal justice, although it was unclear whether the Gonja executions were public. Since her ultimate fate lay in the hands of the divisional chief, it was a valid conclusion that her death symbolized the elimination of an enemy of the state rather than a mere violator of village norms (Goody, pp. 212ff.).

The Trouble with Evil

So far that drawn from ethnographic accounts pictures working or effective methods of the social control for witchcraft and sorcery. Such accounts often, if not typically, present an ideal pattern of control, in many instances phrased in a manner that confuses fact and belief. They convey the trouble with witchcraft and sorcery but omit indications of trouble in efforts at their control; it seldom is discussed in its own right as a variable influence on the actions of those implicated in witchcraft and sorcery.

Douglas (1970) more than any other ethnographer wrote of the inconclusiveness of struggles to control sorcery in African communities, as well as the awareness of their members themselves of the havoc wrought in social relationships by accusations of sorcery and sanctioning by imprisonment or expulsion. In part this was due to the official banning of the use of poison oracles, which in the group Douglas studied, was administered to the accused rather than to a chicken, Azande style. Arrest and imprisonment of an accused sorcerer produced no enduring solutions to conflicts, since his return to his village revived old fears and antagonisms. The same was true for the informal eviction of sorcerers from the Lela community (p. 135).

Each time a supposed sorcerer was chased away, his removal left a legacy of enmity between his supporters and accusers that was not automatically canceled by his eviction.

While Kluckhohn was not as emphatic on the point as Douglas, he nevertheless concluded that witchcraft was socially and psychologically costly to the Navaho in terms of the stresses it created. In many cases its control did more to promote fear and timidity than it did to relieve tensions (1944, p. 121).

Accommodations to Deviance

Indications are that far more persons aroused suspicion of witchcraft and sorcery than met with trial or formal accusation and ultimate execution. Kluckhohn found that of five hundred living Navaho he studied, nineteen had been accused (through gossip) of witchcraft. Ten dead individuals had been accused, and in thirty years only six public accusations or "trials" took place, with two witches executed. Selby (1974, p. 108) could find only one account of a past witch assassination by Zapotec villagers. He identified eighty persons as reputed witches in a village of twelve hundred persons. Whiting (1950, p. 18) was able to idenify "eight or nine" sorcerers among a Paiute settlement of two hundred persons in Oregon, although she noted that the specific accusations changed with passing time and that nearly everyone was a sorcery suspect at some time or another.

Short of execution, accused witches had their houses torched and their crops destroyed, were deprived of cooperative help in cattle husbandry, and generally excluded from informal communication with others. Sometimes people applied pressure to wives or close relatives to withdraw from any social relationships with the accused. In some instances near neighbors moved away from the person marked as witch, but mostly the community sought to exclude or expel the accused.

Lineages in some societies, such as the Mandari, carried a stigma based on standing beliefs and perpetuated by gossip the idea that witchery descended from father to son. In such a case a history of deviance, such as theft, confirmed the witch status to others. For the Paiutes of Oregon, a family's reputation for being mean persons increased the likelihood of accusations (Whiting, 1950). The interaction of suspects with others took on a spurious quality, the general nature of which was described in an article on paranoia (Lemert, 1972, ch. 15). In a real sense they lived in a special psychic environment replete with the conditions conducive to secondary deviance (Lemert, 1972, ch. 3). So we read an excerpt from Buxton (1963, p. 199) exampling such interaction:

Suspects are always incriminating themselves since their neighbors tend to put a sinister interpretation on their actions. Sensing an atmosphere, they restrict their mobility. The fact that their lives are more apart is held to be further proof against them . . . they are frightened to wander about because they know if something happens after their visit they may be killed; they may have no friends and often sit alone. . . . There is careful avoidance but never direct ostracism . . . in general the line is courtesy without intimacy.

Positive Aspects of a Witch Identity

Not all witchcraft suspects acted like beleaguered deviants; some tacitly exploited their imputed role, or at least impressed ethnographers that such was true. Selby (1974, p. 186) tells of an employer of labor who preferred being feared as a witch by workers and made no effort to dispel the belief because it made their management easier. V. Turner (1967) wrote about quarreling that took place over the distribution of meat in Ndemba hunting bands of Northern Rhodesia. This was endemic, due to secret division of spoils that led to jealousy, envy, and hatred of the hunters, who became objects of magical cursing and insinuations of sorcery. The hunters revelled in their bad reputations "much like successful business men" and were unmoved by curses.

Moving halfway around the world to New Guinea one finds people, the Abelam, who spoke quite openly of sorcerers in their midst, primarily because of their political importance. These people likewise recognized the existence of witches, who were exclusively women, but assigned them little importance and never accused them of evildoing despite the belief that they were responsible for half of the infant deaths in this society. In contrast to their African counterparts these women were said at times to act as "good witches" and received pay for their services to wounded warriors, allegedly carried out by turning into rodents that extracted splinters and dirt from their wounds (Forge, 1970, pp. 267ff.).

The given knowledge about African witches, in contrast to that about those of Europe and England, was that accused persons seldom confessed to their supposed roles. However, the ascription of power to witches suggests that under some circumstances it had inherent attractions for persons with marginal status, such as polygamous wives in patrilineal lineages, who often were treated as suspect outsiders. Le Vine (1963, p. 228) offers evidence, some of it hearsay to be sure, that women among the Gusii may actually have aspired to become witches and even sought instruction in witchery from others. Some reputedly confessed to their evil intentions and acts when Christian Pentecostal meetings in their areas offered the opportunity.

Middleton (1963, p. 273) also notes that because of the belief in the latent power of witches certain adult men among the Lugbara "wish it to be believed that they can practice witchcraft" because "a man wishes to be important and to be feared by others." It is also true that witch-cleansing cults recurrent in Africa since the nineteenth century exerted great pressure on alleged witches to confess. Those who did so, after downing medicines, resumed their place in the community without any ostracism (Willis, in Parkin, 1985, ch. 6).

Normative Social Control

Confronted by data indicating that what happened to persons accused of witchcraft in Africa and native American societies range widely from a small number of brutal assassinations to personal avoidance or "leaving the field" by moving away from a suspected evildoer, the idea that individuals learned specific normative responses from fear of being thought a witch must be further questioned if not rejected outright. I prefer to think that the effects of witchcraft accusations and their outcomes in African and mid-American primitive societies were problematic in that any moral influence they may have had lay in the acquisition of knowledge about what happened in real-life situations between accuser and accused and more specifically, how the community dealt with both.

What parents taught their children about witches and how they did it remains obscure in African witchcraft literature. Undoubtedly children in many African societies acquired fear of witches that persisted into adulthood. Most likely the fear merged with the fear of the dark, learned symbolically rather than through experience. Le Vine (1963), who gave a pointed discussion of the matter, said that children of the Gusii learned at an early age that dark is dangerous. Parents reprimanded them if they went out at night and warned them that hyenas might devour them. Since the children never explored the dark, their fears necessarily rested on what they heard or perceived from the behavior of their parents. In other words, as had been true in our society, Gusii witches were born of fantasy rather than from experience.

Such fantasy may well have been associated with the way in which Gusii parents handled aggression in their children. They disapproved of violence, but this repressed rather than eliminated interpersonal hostility, shown by its emergence among adults with alcohol intoxication and its expression in backbiting, malicious gossip and litigation. Witchcraft accusations fit into the same category, but according to Le Vine, took shape in fantasy aggression.

A comparable concern with aggression among children and its repression was a prime consideration for Paiute parents, who whipped siblings who fought. Parents also intimidated children with threats that an owl or a wild beast would carry them off if they disobeyed. Undoubtedly Paiute children observed the connection between fighting and sorcery accusations despite the action of parents who took them away from the scene when fighting broke out among adults—"lest sorcery be thrown around" (Whiting 1950, pp. 70ff.).

The only study I could find exclusively bearing on the theory that witchcraft beliefs engendered conformity lest one be thought a witch, dealt with beliefs of the Bangwa tribe in the area of Africa formerly known as Cameroon. There children, called Children of the Sky, were accused of witchcraft as well as adults, in some cases when they were no more than babies, or even before birth. Evidence came from autopsies, symptoms of illness, dreams, other people's confessions, and the child's own confession made as early as five or six years. A child with certain symptoms, such as jaundice, was urged to confess, and sometimes did so with a rich and lurid imagery, having to do with his misadventures as a bush soul, including, for example, eating another child that stuck in his throat.

Parents, relatives, and others reacted strongly to child confessions; depending on the situation they ostracized the child, drove him from the living compound, or considered putting him to death. However, much ambiguity as well as open conflict clouded such situations. A sick witchchild put in the hospital became the center of much attention and received ritual cures, along with a special diet of chicken protein. Visitors to the sickroom directed numerous searching questions to the child and urged him to confess.

While all of this must certainly have confused if not traumatized a small child, nevertheless some children apparently enjoyed confessing horrible details of their bush experiences (Brain, 1970, p. 170):

> They are little exhibitionists, who know how to play the system, stopping short at the mention of serious crimes.

Bangwa children had full opportunity to learn witchcraft beliefs of adults, which they embellished with a vivid imagery of their own, based on direct experience. They attended witchcraft exorcism rituals; diviners sometimes singled them out for accusation and they heard their parents accused of evil, some of whom endured the poison ordeal in their presence. Children also witnessed witch smelling rites and listened to gruesome tales of shape changing. Sometimes, along with parents, they stood over the corpse of a child and swore their own innocence.

Because of its exotic and fantastic nature, it is not easy to assess such reported material; but on its face it scarcely argues for a theory that witchcraft beliefs produced normative social control since, for one thing, children did not confess to serious crimes. More likely, children in these situations acquired contradictory beliefs about witchery. They realized that anyone might be accused and that under some conditions being accused and confessing accrued rewards that could be exploited for political purposes as well—as when chiefs learned who their malefactors were from the child's confession.

In broad terms it would be difficult to show that African children learned specific norms of behavior lest they be thought witches because it ignores the capacity or inclination of individuals to draw their conclusions from a variety of sources: witch gossip, observing disputes, the disagreements, and partisanship that invested the accusatory process and its outcomes.

My best inference is that what children and adults ultimately learned about witchcraft in African societies was a form of prudence—that one should look out for his or her safety, particularly in ambiguous situations and in the presence of certain persons. This required judgment and decisions about what was dangerous and what was not. The ambiguity surrounding accusations of witchcraft worked against purely stereotyped thinking and shifted attention from such things as norms or what was "right" to predictable and unpredictable behavior (Hoebel, 1968, Postulate IX, p. 70). To say that tribal peoples sought to avoid "the stigma of nonconformity" lest they became suspect as witches is less convincing to me than to say that they, like most people eveywhere, tried to meet their obligations to others and avoid contact with deviant or alienated persons lest trouble arise. Cited statements by indigenous informants on the matter are conspicuously absent from the literature. I was able to locate only two such references. One by an African follows (*Africa*, 1935, p. 514):

> When I was a child I was told that one of two wives of my mother's brother was possessed by a witch, and I was advised to behave well towards her, lest she do me harm. I also avoided her children.

The other reference was to the statement of a teenage Pueblo boy riding with an ethnographer who told him that a certain hill had a reputation for evil and that he "preferred to stay clear of such places" (Simmons, 1974, p. 1).

The Indeterminacy of Social Control

Two ethnographers, Le Vine and Crawford, countered the prevailing theory of those who believed that fear of accusations of witchcraft and being thought to be a witch sustained social norms. Le Vine (1963, pp. 229ff.) called attention to the consequences of the oversight inhered in the writing style of many reports on the subject, in essence the use of the indicative mood to describe phenomena that are necessarily hypothetical, i.e., beliefs. He warned against accepting ethnographic interpretations of witchcraft as "real events" or events about which community consensus existed:

> the secrecy surrounding witchcraft and sorcery prevents the attainment of consensus in particular cases and favors individual intepretations colored by subjective motivations . . . others in the community may not accept his [the accuser's] interpretation of events, their own beliefs in the matter being influenced by their personal emotions, their moral views and their estimations of the accuser and the accused. The contradictory interpretations may lead to social conflict and eventually to a disruptive qurrel in which both cognitive and social conflicts must be resolved.

Crawford (1967, ch. xxi) raised a more fundamental question as to why human beings conform, a question for which he found no simple answer. One of his main points was that the type of conduct leading to accusations of wizardry was not the kind singled out as being actionable wrongs among the Shona. At the same time he stated that this is a class of conduct that rural communities throughout the world control whether or not they believe in wizardry. From his specific inquiries on the subject (unique in the literature), informants made it clear that it was public opinion, "what people say and think," that mainly, and often consciously, formed their views and influenced their attitudes.

Crawford did, however, qualify this conclusion to say that sorcery can be an important sanction to enforce contractual and quasi-contractual obligations. This suggests the existence of some kind of universalistic value underlying social conrol, that which Malinowski (1926) featured as reciprocity and that which Gouldner (1960) later elevated to the status of a norm of reciprocity, presumably universal to human cultures.

Crawford concluded that for the Shona, beliefs in wizardry served more importantly as a means to manipulate public opinion than as a sanction against antisocial conduct. Accusations of such evil work most frequently appeared between persons in sexual, economic, or political competition. By such means individuals appealed to the moral feelings of community members in an effort to involve them in the issue at hand.[2] This often had a spurious quality in that accusations could most easily be made against an unpopular competitor. The reasons for the appeal depended on the person making it and the events of the moment (p. 281).

Courting public opinion and securing involvement of the community in interpersonal conflicts, "getting people to take sides," is something by no means simply done wherever it occurs. This is especially evident when fateful consequences are in the offing for the accused. Generally speaking, human beings tend to be conservative in specific instances about delegating or supporting punitive actions by others acting in their name.

Credence is lent this view by Parkin's (1985, p. 227) general observation that there is much indeterminacy, indecision, and hesitancy in defining particular acts or persons as evil through collective action. People tend to suspend judgments, seek their own confirmation and even feel indignation towards those individuals or regimes—the Pharisees if you will—who claim to know without question what is evil.

Aubert (1985) has written about what he calls *The Hidden Society*, in the course of which he inferentially depicts the feeling states of persons in primitive societies that accompany illness and death attributed to witchcraft and sorcery. He notes that such beliefs are a "two-edged sword," thus reflecting the essentially ambivalent nature of evil experience (p. 169ff.):

---

2. For a complete understanding of witchcraft and social control, heed must be given to the interaction of both the accused and the accuser with others as well as with one another. Intimation of witchcraft can serve many purposes short of open conflict, assassination, or driving someone from the community. In a close-bonded community, for example, one may be totally shamed simply by refusing to conform with prevailing opinion that so-and-so is a witch who made others ill. Seemingly playful references to stew as poisoned may set in course a whole chain of events. Petty plots and counterplots resting on presumed acts of witchcraft wax and wane; some, however, reflecting and revolving around long-standing hostilities or grudges. The dynamic nature of the interaction surrounding occasions of witchcraft has been described by Laura Bohannon 1964, chs. 16 and 17.

illness and death may be viewed as a consequence of sin or black magic or sorcery on the part of someone else. This theory is a two-edged sword. It makes people afraid of incurring enemies because enemies may give them disease through sorcery, and also they are afraid lest their enemies fall sick and accuse them of sorcery. Because the serious offender and the blameless citizen stand equal chances of being sanctioned, one can't teach right and wrong, but can only reinforce it . . . . This creates a feeling of uncertainty and fear of doing anything since no one knows what it takes to release supernatural sanctions. Since everyone has sinned and are aware of something for which they could be punished . . . any sickness or accusations of sorcery may confirm the sick person's theory.

A final commentary emphasizes the general nature of collective social control through intervention in closed corporate communities; very seldom and only incidentally did agents of such control seek to enforce norms in the style of Western justice. It is very doubtful which values that peoples of Western culture apotheosize, "equality, liberty, and justice for all," stood very high in the value scheme of African villagers studied during the colonial period any more than they did among the Comanche, the Eskimo, or the Zapotec. Among the latter according to Nader (1969) intervention in disputes was cautious and pragmatic, mediators seeking in one way or another to restore some kind of working harmony in the community, "to make a balance"—an idea also put forth by Foster (1967, ch. 6) as an equilibrium of social relationships. Such a balance, far from being symmetrical, achieved harmony because it worked, not because it sustained an absract norm or rule or custom such as avoidance of adultery or incest.

This is not to say that values, beliefs and rules—even social structures—did not enter into actions taken towards a person accused of witchcraft. They did so as influences on choice—important in some instances, not in others; important to some persons, not to others; important because some people are present, but also important because they are absent.[3]

---

3. I stated this position in my article, "Issues in the Study of Deviance," *Sociological Inquiry* (1930).

Heuristic Analysis

Heuristic analysis of social contol and witchcraft as problematical
gains favor over that conceived by theory and hypotheses from
the fact that ethnographic research on African witchcraft and
sorcery, going clear back to Evans-Pritchard (1937), took place
during an epoch of imperialistic conquest that brought significant socioeconomic and sociolegal changes to the continent.
Yet cognizance of such intrusive influences by the theoretically
oriented ethnographers of the time at best was only residual
or appended.

Kluckhohn's (1967) research on witchcraft came closest to
dynamic analysis that incorporated strands of the critical historical
method of American anthropology. Likewise, Selby (1974), in his
study of witchcraft as deviance, took care to account for a kind
of pristine pattern of witchcraft among his Zapotec villagers by
referring to the historical circumstances in Oaxaca that allowed
it to escape the onerous influence of the hacienda system.

By 1972 a study of witchcraft among the Pedi people of South
Africa (Sansom, 1972, ch. 5) confronted the facts of socioeconomic
change in an heuristic mode, showing with concepts derived
from his data how the "tempo of sociation" essentially eliminated the basis for community validation of witchcraft accusations. The volatile social relationships in the chiefdom induced
by labor migration and the absence of men led to uncertainty
of support among the chief's followers and worked against the
formation of structured groups and public opinion. This made
witchcraft accusations risky for the accuser lest his charges be
seen as no more than mischievous, vindictive, or the unbalanced
expression of personal feelings. The opinion vacuum limited
the accuser to consultation with a *Ngata*, a doctor of magic,
an act that became public knowledge but kept secret the subject
for consultation. A state of pluralistic ignorance plus the inference that the person doing the consulting may have obtained
some new magic for his purposes put people on notice, particularly since, following Aubert's (infra, pp. 66, 67) line, some
would feel particularly vulnerable due to past transgressions.

However, I believe Aubert overstated the matter in another
respect by leaving the impression that fear of magical aggression

had a paralyzing effect on members of the community. Much better to see an underlying process in which balanced perceptions and feelings in an ongoing interpersonal context produced caution rather than heavy deterrence. In modern society this can best be seen in the effects created by the sudden appearance of a police patrol car on freeway traffic speeds by motorists in contrast to the far less predictable effects of posted speed limits or other symbols of legal rules.

The Homeostatic Model of Social Control and Beyond

Some years ago when the world was young I wrote a piece on "The Folkways and Social Control" (Lemert, 1942) mainly criticizing the tendency of sociologists to reify the term, but also making a distinction between passive and active social control. My argument for recognizing the existence of the latter, active social control, reflected my then more sanguine view of the human capacity to shape the course of social change. I left the idea of passive social control largely undeveloped—as a kind of sop for the followers of William Graham Sumner (1906), whose ultraconservative thought flowed from a storehouse of lore about primitive and rural societies.

My latter-day exposure to anthropological field data on witchcraft and sorcery gave me pause for a backward look at passive social control, which for Sumner meant a kind of automatic coercion of the individual by folk usages. This idea, common to earlier anthropology, stated as unreflective compliance with "immemorial custom" (Hartland, 1924, p. 138) finally ran athwart Malinowski's demonstration of the dynamic processes that sustained compliance with ritual economic exchanges among the Trobriand islanders (Malinowski, 1926). Granting that Malinowski erred in a number of his interpretations of crime control among the Trobriands (Hoebel, 1968, ch. 8), nonetheless his general viewpoint helped to validate a more dynamic view of law and society for anthropological study.

As an early spokesman for "functionalism" Malinowski (1926, pp. 92ff.) portrayed sorcery as a chief's means of social control that ingrained a wholesome fear of punishment and retribution among the Trobriander fishermen and yam growers. Hoebel reinterpreted Malinowski's data to propose that the alliance between the ruling chief and his sorcerer savored of tyranny and that Trobriander subjects "fought back" with their own ready magic. Conflict rather than ready compliance with authority made social order problematical rather than a fixed consequence of official sorcery.

Of course, the fact that conflict based on competing sorceries existed among the Trobrianders did not in itself negate a functionalist or structural interpretation of social control, which became the "orthodoxy of the 1950s" (Douglas, 1970, p. xxi). For anthropologists of the time, conflict restored homeostasis in society by provoking social control and effectively reorganizing it. The model in use came from biology, which gave prominence to the concept of system and equilibrium of forces (Henderson, 1970; Parsons, 1952). The violence of witchcraft accusations and assassinations became part of a self-correcting system that facilitated the release of aggression and then put society back into working order.

Douglas (1970, p. xxv) sharply criticized this model but concluded that, shorn of its crudities, it could be made serviceable:

Take away the rigidity and crudity of the homeostatic control model and it still provides an explanatory framework based on the idea of a communication system.

Unfortunately, Douglas' break with structural analysis, on close scrutiny, proved to be more apparent than real since she replaced a social system with a communication system having overtones of *cybernetics*, although she did not use this term. She reified the witch, then led the reader through diagrammed scenarios in which community members socially defined the witch as an external or internal enemy together with various functions that corresponded to the definitions. Communication about witchcraft varied, but with a limited number of meanings and above all "according to variations on structure" (p. xxvi).

Despite this ingenuity, Professor Douglas left the reader disappointed because while she seemed to make room for human choice in her analysis, ultimately she concluded that meanings are produced by structures. Moreover, her concern remained with beliefs and symbols rather than interaction; and she perpetuated the eerie quality of writing about witches in the indicative mood characteristic of mid-century African studies of the subject. Here and there in her discourse one gets a glimpse of people; but generally they recede behind beliefs, "ascribed roles," and "sparse social relations." At most Douglas warned against a "too rigid social determinism" in the study of sorcery and witchcraft.

Prudence, Balance, and Social Control

I now turn to an interpretation of sorcery as a means of social control most consistent with heuristic method, featuring ideas of symbolic interaction and choices as affected by considerations of costs of action. Costs here are conceived as cultural and personal values are necessarily sacrificed in order to sustain or satisfy other values (Lemert, 1981).

Such an analysis must somehow cope with the confusion between sorcery and witchcraft rampant in the literature on the subjects. Setting aside witchcraft, for reasons I hope are now clear, I prefer to think of sorcery as the use of power to work harm against others, best put as *negative charisma*. The power of sorcery is distinguished by its attribution by others to identifiable members of a community, not power given to fantasized witches, whose identity must be established by gossip and accusations. Generally speaking, or as I speak here, sorcerers occupied statuses and played specialized roles in actual communities: as curers, shamans, witch doctors, medicine men, magicians, diviners, seers, wise persons, and witch finders. While such persons were deemed to have monopolized mystical means of power, it is also true that ordinary persons could have access to such power either directly, as through dreams, or by using folk medicines or by hiring a sorcerer. The power of sorcery came from the use of material objects, such as a medicine horn, or from medicines, accompanied by or enhanced by rituals.

The prudence-balance model of social control works by a kind of negative reciprocity in which one person is deterred from aggressing socially against another by awareness of the immediate power to retaliate with unpleasant or costly consequences. At the same time should an individual become a victim of an injurious attack, he/she could strike back with sorcery of his/her own. From this comes a rough cumulative balance or balances of "power" serving to maintain a state of accommodation if not genuine civility in interpersonal relationships. The balance in question is not an exchange in rational utilitarian terms but rather the result of evaluations in which costs and gains are physically, psychologically, and culturally defined. Feedback, the perception of the consequences of prior choices and decisions, also significantly influences the decisions whether and what kind of retaliation is pursued.

People of the closed corporate community, my reference point for discussion, followed few norms in the sense of substantive rules—sometimes no more than shared understandings as to what was best to do in instances of murder, incest, or endangering a common food supply. Even these were understood primarily as interindividual problems, with group or community involvement of secondary importance. The rule inhered in the remedy, or put more precisely, the rule was the remedy. Acts that today we know as crimes against abstract entities like the State, in simple, low-energy societies of the past, were personal wrongs—or to use legalese, *torts*—and were so treated for the most part. Gillen (1934) gave the almost classic example of such with his description of reactions to trouble among the Barama River Caribs.

Sorcery and Social Control
Among the Yokuts-Mono

The natives here cited as an exemplar of a prudence-balance type of social control lived in villages in central California, organized in patrilineages under a tribal chief. Their cosmology was expressed through designated influences of totem birds and animals. Apart from the chief, ranking persons consisted of shamans, subchiefs, messengers, dance managers, and spokesmen. A "trickle down" share-the-wealth ethos marked the culture, whose values were implemented through the chief, who as keeper of the storehouses dispensed food and assistance to the poor, the widowed, and the aged. The chief also engaged in trade as well as receiving gifts for staging dances and rituals. In essence he collected taxes ceremonially; he also served as a fatherly consultant and gave his sanction for a rudimentary self-help type of justice.

The chief helped to settle some but not all quarrels and sometimes intervened in feuds. However, all cases of murder and serious assault came before him; and he specifically authorized revenge, after which supposedly there could be no further retaliation. The same held true when the chief pronounced an individual to be a public enemy. However, there were instances when an angry man consulted venerable elders and bypassed the chief in seeking revenge.

Note that these California natives had no laws, such as against the theft of food, made unnecessary by a working welfare system. The only understanding shared by all the tribal members which approximated law was that of a "life for a life." The author of the study paraphrased here called their way of life a practical political scheme providing for the needs of the majority not on humanitarian grounds but in terms of their unique values (Gayton, 1930, p. 407). The culture of the Yokuts-Mono ranked low in complexity even for native Californian cultures, which relative to others of the world were known for their simplicity. Relative to law, the Yokuts-Mono closely resembled the primitive anarchy of the Eskimos.

Integration and order in Yokuts-Mono society rested upon interpersonal amity, based on personal character. The sense of right and wrong was instilled in the socialization process by parents and neighbors. The components of character were values: truthfulness, modesty in regard to one's self, and, above all, generosity. Yokuts-Mono people did not learn about rules, norms, and laws; they learned how to behave towards one another. This is learned to a greater or lesser degree in all societies.

But the Yokuts, like the rest of human beings, had troubles, misunderstandings, quarrels, divorces, fights, assaults, and murders motivated by anger, hatred, and envy—the inevitable consequences of ambivalence peculiar to close and intimate social interaction. What then served as the ultimate guarantee of social order and reasonable individual security in this society?

The control or influence looming in the background of Yokuts-Mono life was sorcery, which on balance worked for the public good. More precisely it was the fear of sorcery, an influence with no legal or formal basis but nevertheless an awe-inspiring force used by chiefs through shamans. Individuals also could use sorcery as a weapon for their protection, the awareness of which invested the socializing process and acted in the immediate situation to deter wrongdoing. The author (Gayton, p. 409) pictured the influence of sorcery as follows:

> A man dared not cheat another at gambling or trading, commit adultery, or neglect any civil or ceremonial duty towards his neighbor, lest the offended person visit sickness or death upon him or some member of his family, either by his own power or that of a shaman hired for the purpose. On the other hand a man could not take offense for no reason for the matter would be aired before the chief.

Of course, circumstances or personality problems could and did lead to trouble among the Yokuts-Mono. Some of this came from the ubiquitous temptation to misuse occult power or from suspicions that this was the case. While most shamans did their best to cure illness and admitted their failures, not so for others. Some continued to "cure" patients for long periods, leading to suspicions that they caused the illness to make money. Sexual harassment was not unknown to shamans. Some of them sought to exploit the fears they instilled by sexually appropriating young, nubile girls and when rebuffed, sought revenge by directing their "magic" against the girls' families to make them sick. At times evil shamans extorted property by threats.[4]

---

4. Among the Tlingit Indians sorcery was reported to be subject to considerable abuse. According to informants, persons caught in the act of sorcery suffered immediate execution, notably by his own clansmen. Usually hired shamans named such evildoers. Thieves sometimes claimed they had been bewitched by a slave and thus escaped penalty. Men of high rank and great wealth could by paying a shaman commit crimes with impunity, also eliminate rivals by having a shaman name them as murderers (Oberg, 1934).

Gluckman (1965, p. 233) asserted that the belief that a "good magician" may use his power nefariously at the request of a client or a chief was/is widespread in Africa, Asia, Melanesia, and North America.

This suggests that those seeking a substantive conception of evil may find it in the corruption of power where or when it can be monopolized.

Chiefs typically formed alliances with shamans for socially beneficial purposes. If an affluent tribal person failed to make contributions for important ceremonies this put a heavier burden on others. The chief then might call in a shaman, who, according to belief, made the shirker ill. He then treated him and took payments that he divided with the chief. In this way the chief more or less forced compliance with the expectation of generosity, which allowed him to share wealth and care for persons less able to support themselves. However, it was also true that chiefs connived with their shamans to carry out inter-tribal killings.

Shamans seemed to enjoy a privileged position by monopolizing a good deal of power, and the same could be said of chiefs. However, a rough accountability kept both in check. The shaman who misused his power was at risk of "discovery" and sudden death—an eventuality supported by anecdotal evidence in a case in which a shaman was rebuffed by a young girl. All members of the family except the girl and her father became ill and died; then the daughter grew sick, presumably due to the anger of the shaman. So after obtaining sanction of the chief the father waylaid the shaman (Gayton, 1930, p. 392):

> Cahaola was waiting on the trail . . . hidden. Then he saw
> Puea . . . riding a white horse . . . very drunk. As he came
> opposite Cahoala jumped up and shot him through the
> body . . . Puea fell off the horse . . . admitted the crime
> and said he was glad he was going to be killed. Then
> Cahaola shot him between the eyes.

When a chief made bad decisions or exploited his position for self-serving ends it soon became known to others. No one tried to depose him; rather he lost prestige and his public following, as people shifted their allegiance to another chief. Hence he had more to lose than gain by inequitable decisions and secret machinations.

The author of this study made a point similar to that made by Evans-Pritchard about the attitudes of the Azande towards the dangers of witchcraft, namely that the Yokuts and Western Mono did not live in continual anxiety and dread because of the threat of sorcery hanging over them. They dealt with the threat as a commonplace feature of their lives, not unlike modern motorists who speed along the freeways with the awareness of possible injury or death from accidents. Low-lying anxieties, of course, quickly rose to the surface as they got pained, shocked, or traumatized by illnesses, death, and other misfortunes.

Some Interim Conclusions

One of the significant problems left by the interpretations of witchcraft and sorcery of mid-century ethnographers, especially in Africa, was their commitment to a substantive idea of evil, plainly stated by Evans-Pritchard as a prototype in which one person motivated by hatred carried out a planned assault on another. Others with his interests elaborated this isomorphic view of evil by designating witches as abominations, as totally, grossly, and inexcusably immoral. An inescapable question remains as to whether the natives themselves personified witches in this way or whether ethnographers did so, by definition making witches antisocial.

Harwood (1970, p. 71), writing towards the end of the witchcraft research era, registered his dissent from the accepted perspective on witches. By shifing attention from the persona of witches to the stated nature of their power, with care and attention given to the translation of native linguistic terms, he concluded that they were morally neutral:

> Nganga like itonga seems to be a neutral power which can be used to effect both moral and immoral ends. On the one hand it may be used to detect and control malevolent peoples with mystical power; on the other it may be used anti-socially to sicken or kill one's enemies.

Bloomhill (1962, pp. 30ff.) makes the same kind of assertion about the dual use of power: "This power [of the African witch] is due to the same despotic might of belief in the supernatural that makes it possible for the nganga to allay the people's fears." Further support for this interpretation comes from accounts of the Tiv and the Nandi peoples (Harwood, 1970, p. 74).

Shifting attention from witchcraft and sorcery *per se* to the concept of power brings feelings and motives of individuals into a more realistic alignment with beliefs. It also enlightens social control as something that people do rather than that which is done to them by abstract beliefs or by the ineluctable working of a social structure. While it is true that beliefs provide a large contextual background for social control, people nevertheless experience evil in an interactional process replete with feelings that sort out beliefs and that constrain or drive actions.

In the panoramic background of social control, community groups, by definition small and centripetally integrated, are sideline or late entry participants in the process. Here social structure and personalities influence group interaction that must generate power by consensus necessary to validate action taken against witches and sorcerers.

The illustrative case of the Yokuts-Mono made it clear that the natives in question attributed the malicious use of power to evil motives rather than to power itself. Thus it was the "mean" shamans or corrupt chiefs who did so. That the same kind of power they used could be invoked to defend one's self against sorcery further strengthens the idea of neutral power converted to good or evil ends. Finally, take note that Paiutes believed that if power was put to evil uses it redounded to the subject's misfortune, causing sickness. Hence power for them had an integrity and mystique of its own.

Passive social control in large part consisted of behavioral constraints based on fear of others' sorcery, but it may be that the report on Yokuts-Mono social control overemphasized the scope of deviance controlled by this fear. As I have tried to show, in a number of tribal societies assassinations for witchcraft and sorcery counted few in comparison to the numbers of those who were accused. Very likely more murders took place over adultery, theft of cattle, or gambling debts than for witchcraft.

Whiting (1950) could find no history of killings of Paiute sorcerers, and only a few suffered expulsion. However, gossip about sorcerers abounded and helped to discharge hostile feelings, as well as putting such feelings into perspective from the feedback other gossipers provided, the accused included. The ethnographer of the Paiutes pointed to another possibly more generic basis of constraint on aggression or deviance, namely the fear of physical retaliation, which she named as the most important regulatory mechanism for these people (p. 78):

> Murder, adultery, theft and nonfulfillment of obligations, then, are all offenses for which a person can expect physical revenge. The death penalty is considered just retaliation for murder but is considered too severe for other offenses. Assault or destruction of property is considered appropriate punishment for these.

It is fair to say that one of the most important troubles with social control in small, closed societies was how to limit retaliation. Some societies, such as the Eskimos, had no solution for the problem. Other peoples sought to restrain victims of aggression through social pressures to accept compensation in lieu of revenge, with the aim of forestalling feuds and preventing large-scale destruction of life and property. In the final analysis in which controls succeeded, the entire community acted as an informal court of opinion, putting pressures on relatives and families, who in turn restrained their offended kin.

While they are not entirely clear on the issue, sources generally hold that killings of witches did not lead to claims for compensation. One possible explanation of this was that sorcery was simply murder by another name so that the "life for a life" rule justified retaliation. But this would not account for killings in which the sorcerer or witch merely caused sickness or loss of cattle or crops. This clouds any universalistic idea of a necessary equation of punishments with the seriousness of offenses. What was it, then, that gave witchery and sorcery their special qualities, qualities that are troublesome for the anthropology of law? Moore (1972) in her discussion of legal liability in tribal societies excluded these from her discussion on grounds of their ambiguity. This more or less aligned her thought with that of African ethnographers that witchcraft stood for feelings and actions unamenable to legal control and direct punitive sanctions.

Despite Moore's reservations I see no reason why her characterization of the circumstances under which tribal communities

or their constituent groups used direct punishments: (1) grossness of the offense; (2) recurrent offenses, i.e., recidivism and
recusance; are not applicable for understanding social reactions
to witchcraft and sorcery, particularly if the focus is on social
rather than legal control.

Grossness of an offense may lie in its obvious features, such
as a gruesome murder. What may make lesser offenses seem
gross to others and lead to strong punishments as in the case
of witchcraft is the imputation of insidiousness and connotations of entrapment, beguilement, and treachery. The association of insidiousness with night, darkness, and surreptition
greatly influenced the imputed nature of wichcraft. Such features
also mark such crimes as burglary and rape, apparent, for example,
in penal codes that recognize nighttime burglary as more
aggravated than if committed during the day.

Moore's (1972) difficulties in subsuming witchcraft in her
offense liability analysis could have benefited had she drawn
on more dynamic ideas of deviance theory, specifically to
recognize that offenders get typified by others and that the
marshalled influence of a society or community in the social
control process is variable rather than constant. Grossness of
an offense may well lie in its "successful" definition as such
rather than in some ascertainable differences between offenses.
Douglas (1970, p. xxv), using the idiom of communication
theory, cogently described how the community under collective
stresses reaches an emotionally charged consensus and by word
and action defines a person or persons as witches:

> People are trying to control one another albeit with small
> success. The idea of the witch is used to whip their own
> consciences or those of their friends. The witch image
> is as effective as the idea of the community is strong.

Just how or why communities generate high levels of
emotion or a "climate of opinion" favorable to violent action
against an individual—such as the suspected witch—has never
been satisfactorily explained by students of collective behavior.
The accusatory process in regards to witchcraft has been variously
described but usually in formal terms, making reference to unusual

incidents, quarrels, retrospective redefinition of events and persons, pooling of opinions, and validation by one with occult powers. Whiting (1950, p. 64ff.) indicated five factors or steps in the process by which a Paiute got stigmatized as a sorcerer: (1) an accusation of meanness or "having bad thoughts"; (2) gossip in which the accused has few partisans or defenders; (3) circumstantial evidence, such as threats followed by someone's death; (4) sanction by a doctor; (5) reaction of the accused by fleeing, confessing, or ignoring the allegation.

This kind of formal analysis of the process loses the often present ambiance of evil and leaves it empty of the powerful emotions afoot. Hence I add a sixth factor, namely the culmination of background fears, such as those resulting from numerous unexplained deaths in a community or a known epidemic coming near, best exampled in Laura Bohannon's fictionalized account *Return to Laughter* (1964, ch. 20) in which she writes of the "water," a dreaded synonym for smallpox claiming daily victims in the African community she studied. It also seems to be the case that widely fluctuating economic conditions may contribute to changes and the intensification of witchcraft fears derived from cultural ambivalence towards the accumulation of wealth in an intensely egalitarian society (Ardener, 1970).

The Recusant and Social Control

The other way in which practices of tribal peoples differ from those of Anglo-Saxon justice appears in efforts to deal with or control the recusant or the recidivist. In her spin-off references to witchcraft Moore (1970, p. 92) made a final point that many individual expulsions of individuals from the tribal community in the guise of witchcraft actually were for other reasons, to wit, defects of character, deviance, and failure to meet obligations.[5] Granting the wisdom of this, it may be more fitting to say that

---

5. Moore's 1965 speculation is verified by an account of the *Kevais* in the Solomon Islands, where "the clan was happy enough to get rid of [to collect a bounty or to save their own skins]: that is, they were people considered expendable or undesirable: such as, disobedient or wanton girl, an irresponsible young man . . . or one without immediate kin. . . ." Elota's story (1978, p. 66).

the trouble Moore noted was with the unresponsiveness of individuals to informal social control—persuasion, pleading, gossip, and ridicule—which set them apart from others even though they did not commit major offenses.

It is the person typified as a recusant, unrepentant, or without remorse who ultimately is at risk of death or banishment by collective community action (Znaniecki, 1963, p. 347). This is because such individuals, by their demeanor and their recurrent actions and inactions, are perceived and imputed to be enemies of society (Gusfield, 1981). They are seen to defy authority or they become intolerable or unaffordable nuisances who have alienated so many persons or groups that none is left to stay alienating gossip or to intervene in their behalf. Whether the manner, declarations, or acts of the individual actually threaten society or its institutional authority are beside the point because the issue of control overrides all others. The *persona non grata* is troublesome in a cumulative rather than in a substantive sense.

4

The Primitive Witch Hunt

In what follows I try to enlighten with as much contextual detail as possible that which hopefully may emerge as a pattern for further research into the social control of evil, here deemed to be witchcraft and sorcery. In preceding sections I have dealt more or less in passing with reactions of natives driven by fear or panic to execute witches or to expel them from the community. Beyond these "moral panics" one finds accounts of more organized social control, incorporating rituals and specialized personnel of trans-local origins together with their legendary validation. These also qualify as distinctive cultlike social movements come to be known as witch hunts, witch findings, or sometimes witch "cleansing."

The witch hunt in primitive form took shape in Africa, as opposed to Melanesia, where so-called cargo cults, prevailed—movements that in some areas blended with nationalism, such as the Marching Rule movement and the Moro movement in the Solomon Islands (Kent, 1972; Hogbin, 1945).

Despite an available body of literature on primitive witch hunts, they do not appear in general discussions seeking to distinguish and classify primitive cults and social movements. These have been variously classified as revitalization, vitalistic, millenarian, and messianic; whether formal classification of this kind is useful for the study remains unclear. Smith (1959) voiced her misgivings about such efforts in this way:

and it should be added that I see little value in classification for its own sake. The one offered here is meant
to clarify process and aid in its analysis.

Thus while Smith's intimate knowledge of the Shaker movement in the state of Washington made her cogenial to the idea that cults were responses to social and economic dissatisfaction, she was compelled to note that some such movements are not deliberate or conscious (p. 12). However, as will be shown, they may and do include rational economic components. The idiosyncratic features of primitive social movements abound and leave a question as to whether their dissimilarities do not outweigh their similarities. This poses a corollary query about the witch hunt, namely whether there is an associated pattern of social control sufficient to serve as an analytical model for its more general study.

The African Witch Hunt—Early Accounts

The earliest accounts of witch hunts date from the 1930s, although such movements probably hark back to an earlier time, since they were reported to be "widespread all over Africa" at the time (Richards, 1935). Generally speaking such movements originated from an individual within the community, or from scouts or "wonder workers"[1] who came into the village with a magic remedy for human suffering.

In Northern Rhodesia the *Ba Mucampi* were young men dressed in European clothing who worked with local paid assistants. Their inspirational leader was Kamwede of Mlange in Nyasaland. Arriving at the village, the *Ba Mucampi* arranged for the headman to assemble his people, who were lined up in files and marched past the witch finder who used a mirror to detect those he motioned aside to join a group of witch suspects.[2]

---

1. No accepted term is applied to these advance agents, which suggests that they had no common antecedents. The possibility that charlatans were attracted to the idea to exploit its pecuniary possibilities is a strong one. Reference is made to the *Ba Mucampi* as "missionaries" who passed through Bantu country, "who pretended they had been sent from Nyasaland by a woman named 'Maria'." They were put in jail and deported to Nyasaland (Junod, H., 1936, p. 304).

2. Another method of identification found among the Zulus relied on "smelling out a witch," done by a woman, an *isangoma*, who was summoned by the village chief. As the *isangoma* pranced and howled in imitation of wild animals, the audience gave her cues by intense chanting when she sniffed an unpopular person, chanting that "sank to a low mournful note" when a person was well liked (Bloomhill, G. [1962], pp. 56ff.).

Wielders of the mirrors then called on all of the witches to yield up their "horsis," which in actuality were no more than charms most natives had to ward off evil things. Those identified as "witches" then had to drink a little *mucapi* medicine made from red powder that gave the liquid a soapy taste.

By such tactics the *Ba Mucampi* guaranteed no less than the complete elimination of witchcraft from the district. They warned that those who returned to the evil practice of witchcraft after ingesting the medicine would die a horrible death. Those who failed to cooperate would be caught on a visit by the founder of the movement, who, by drum beating, herded the recusants into a graveyard where they were exposed to public gaze.

While the summary given here outlines a very early witch finding movement in most particulars, a further comment drawn from events of a later movement sheds light on its mystical aura of cult leadership. The movement in question appeared in 1952 among Bantu people near Lake Tanganika (Willis, R. G., 1968) and concerned fateful events in the lives of two brothers who had amassed a substantial amount of money. When the older brother died the younger brother returned, and after getting permission, dug up the grave of his brother, in the process of which the corpse sat up and pronounced, "I have come back to rid the world of sorcery." He forthwith branded a man by cuts on his forehead. And so the *Ba Mucampi* movement got its start.

As with the earlier movement, this one brought visitors from outside to local villages where they rubbed medicine into incisions in the forehead of suspected witches. This allegedly guaranteed immunity from the impulse to sorcerize, but it also carried the threat of instant death for those who reverted to the practice. In some cases those refusing to cooperate with the witch finders received beatings.

Divination and Witch Hunts

From what has been related about Azande medicine men previously, it is clear that divination and witch finding are closely associated, even though the diviner's role is generalized. The diviner accordingly can be classed with herbalists, shamans, and medicine men. Park (1963, p. 247) held that divination is an institutionalized pattern that legitimated collective action by contact with ancestors or spirits, done by consulting randomly cast objects or entrails of slain fowls and animals. More specifically this included seeking auguries for hunting success, bounteous crops, and astute political decisions of rulers and war lords. Put simply, the diviner dramatized situations but left the choice of action to others.

The tie between divining and witch finding under some circumstances may have favored the evolution of diviners into leaders of cults. Such was true of one called Chickanga, who in 1960 rose to prominence in Nyasaland, ultimately drawing crowds of people from four African countries (Redmayne, A., 1970). Originally Chickanga served as a diviner but his fame grew, enhanced by a familiar legend that he had died, then risen from the grave with no less of a mission than to clear all Africa of sorcery.

Chickanga's cult differed in that people came to him rather than he or his associates seeking out others. However, he was able to work his way at a distance through local agents and village headmen, using the accepted method of pressuring suspects to confess to sorcery then marking their foreheads with knife cuts. There seems to be no evidence that Chickanga and those working in his cause profited by charging fees, although local natives gained economically from the sale of food to pilgrims who made the long journey necessary to consult with Chickanga.

Like other witch hunting movements, Chickanga's had a short life span of only a few years. Initially people testified to his miraculous cures and spoke of a decline of illness in their areas, due to the fact that all the sorcerers had been summoned to meet with Chickanga. At first people saw no problems with the movement; and it was difficult for local churches to object to practices similar to their own, such as exorcism.

Reaction and resistance to Chickanga's activities and influence ultimately came from a governmental and administrative level. The president of the country ordered Chickanga to move nearer, to live at Blantagne where "he would be watched." This grew out of a complaint by the Presbyterian church that Chickanga's mission stirred up beliefs in witchcraft, undermined the authority of the chiefs, and constituted a public health menace.

The Lenshina Movement

In light of subsequent history of Rhodesia and other states in Africa, the cult movements so far described must be seen as nascent nationalism bearing a potential for revolutionary change. A striking feature of these and other such movements was the differentiation of the role of leaders, including the participation of women called priestesses in some areas. Such was the case with the Lenshina movement, that saw the rise of a kind of Joan of Arc figure, Alice Lenshina, to a paramount position of leadership. Viability of the new cult showed in the speed with which it replaced existing missionary activity, the devotion, fervor, and the loyalty of converts, plus their generous contributions of financial support.

The tendency to deify cult leaders in this account was illustrated by Lenshina's claim to have had a vision of God in 1954, who allegedly handed down explicit commands during several of her death/revival experiences. These were: to work on Earth using a bible he (God) gave her, to sing hymns, and to tell missionaries about her experiences.

Lenshina first leveled tirades against sorcery and witchcraft, in essence calling for a holy war against these evils that, she said: "kills a person made by God," and in ominous colloquial terms likened these to "a lion who catches human beings."

The conspicuous strains of Puritanism in Lenshina's theology appealed to natives who had previously identified with the local Scotch church. She condemned polygyny together with adultery, smoking (hemp), and wearing hats in church. The new faith emerged as a form of Protestantism in an African context. Put more generally, the Lenshina cult proved to Neo-Christian and anti-European, whose "priests" played on Black/White differences. This came to the fore in several incidents of protest against the government and conflict with tribal chiefs.

The Antisorcery Movement as Patterned Social Control

An accepted idea in studies of collective behavior is that cults and sects evolve into institutionalized religion. Such culmination can be found in the history of African conquest states, where social control emanated from a political center or a capital city. An informative instance comes from the account of antisorcery in Nupe society—and African emirate—going back to 1932 (Nadel, S., 1935). Herein social control went beyond mere collection of tribute characteristic of conquest states. It included specialized agency—that of priests with rituals of a secret society that intervened from the outside and that had cultural roots in the capital city as well as in local villages.

The social control of witches took two forms. In one, the simpler of the two, a village chief summoned the suspect, usually an older woman, and demanded that she confess, pay a fine, and save her victim. Part of this procedure required an ordeal of downing medicine that supposedly caused death should the woman return to her evil work. In extreme cases an official master of powerful magic, *Etsu Nupe*, could have a condemned witch beheaded in the public square.

In the second method of social control, sanctioned by the Emir's magic, masked figures—cult members from afar—danced among assembled villagers a day long to single out the witches among them with the help of an "interpreter." In this method the dancers drank medicine rather than the witch suspects, something done to achieve invisibility and the "soul separation" needed to detect the evildoers. On being identified as a witch the woman was taken into the bush and roughly tested to prove her guilt. She could buy her freedom or, lacking the funds, suffered death at the hands of the "spirits."

The outcome of these punitive forays against witches depended on which persons took action. When the local elders made known the witches, the dancing spirits simply appeared and performed their rituals to intimidate them and collect fines. However, when the secret society took charge, its representatives showed up at the king's court to warn in dire terms of the need to curb the witches. Spirit dancers then appeared without warning in the villages causing women to flee into the bush or so frightened them otherwise that they collected money to buy themselves free as a group.

These happenings created general unrest, so much so that women neglected their duties. Coming at harvest time made the situation even more troublesome, causing village chiefs hurriedly to collect large sums of money to buy off the witch finders. This proved to be very lucrative for the *Etsu Master*, who received one third of all such monies, and more so for the secret society, that kept two thirds.

The reader is cautioned that this account of the use of masked dancer rituals as an economic and political control method is historical, since it ended in 1921, prior to the arrival of the ethnographer. Furthermore, I was not able to decipher all of the ambiguities that inhered in the arcane nature of his reported materials.

From a jaundiced view, the methods of social control were no more than crude methods for collecting tribute from sub-servient village peoples. However well such a system may have served in early conquest states, the culture and social organization of the Emirate were such that large-scale exploitation of the population ultimately became self-defeating. This can be inferred from the fact that reverberations of the antiwitch enterprises reached the capitol in 1921 when several accused witches were killed and a trial by law of those involved followed.

The ethnographer (or, should we say historiographer) concluded his study with comments on the "psychological problem," which, he held, inheres in the "idea of witchcraft," namely that evil will always be with us and the best that can be done is to "limit it to a reasonable degree" because of its "unaccountable freedom." Admitting that the principles of protection from evil do not apply is part of "safe guiding laws and protecting principles."

Reduced to its essence, Nadel's conclusion sounds like a scholar's theodicy, that is, there is evidence for both order and disorder in the world. By accepting this fact men are freed from the need for quixotic ventures against evil and can spend their time and energies in more constructive ways. Whether these ideas rest on the data, which depict a massive social disruption, is questionable.

Inasmuch as the evil witches of Nupe were exclusively women, one must concede that there is a perceptible gender aspect to Nadel's argument. Those given to symbolic delving may wonder whether the author is not unwittingly referring to a sexual basis for irrationality, perhaps lamenting the futility of the age-old war of the sexes.

Intended or not, Nadel's way of presenting the issue savors of uncritical acceptance, or at best an advocacy of passive social control of societal troubles in general. Unfortunately this ignores the transcendent nature of evil, which goes beyond ordinary troubles, the intensity of the experience of evil, and the reaction to it. Finally, Nadel blurs the line between the purposes of scientific research and humanistic or social philosophy.

The present study will best focus on the contextual detail within which the drive to eliminate evil transformed into the prime mover of evil itself. However, the social scientist cannot stay content with descriptive details; he/she must go on to some kind of comparative analysis that rises above mere ethnographic reporting. One way of doing this is to compare the summarized studies in order to construct an analytical model applicable to the more general study of antisorcery movements.

Similarities and Differences

While the differences in the antisorcery movements so far described are considerable, the similarities are impressive. These have to do with their origin, leadership, ritual, and organization. Note that in all cases the movements had a mystical religious quality in the sense that some form of spiritual experience and mystical communications mediated their origin and subsequent operation. These ranged from divination to visions and conversations with God.

The origin of leadership was translocal in that legendary events and associated rituals occurred at a distance from persons attracted to the movement. Chickanga devotees traveled to see him rather than his representatives traveling to seek out impressionable followers. In time he created a detached organization that worked through agreements with local chiefs.

In one case not hitherto summarized, among the Ashanti people (Ward, B., 1956) the pattern of anti-witch control diffused indirectly through self-help on the part of a man beset by illness and mechanical troubles with his lorry. He was advised by others to seek protection and salvation from Kune against witches believed to have caused his troubles. This unnamed man bought medicine from a priest in the northern territories. He subsequently sent his nephew there to learn the proper rituals, which involved confessions of witchery, praying and chanting by participants, and the sacrifice of fowls.

The fetish, as it came to be known, spread widely throughout the southern Gold Coast and brought in considerable money from the entrance fees paid by "witches" and "sorcerers." Headmen and elders presently took control and divided the funds for local use among the original owners of the fetish, the "stool" (the village), and a reserve fund to defray communal purchases, such as a lorry.

It is difficult to understand the Ashanti fetish solely by reference to social control. Anyone could become a member simply by paying a fee, taking a bit of a kola, and obeying its rules. These had the sound of the Christian Decalogue: Do not commit adultery; Do not steal; Do not harbor evil thoughts against anyone. However, personal motives for participation had to do with barren women, sick or dying children, impotent men, fear of crop failures, or failure in examinations. All these ills were taken as signs of witchcraft, the elimination of which stood as the overriding concern for fetish members.

Feelings of participants at fetish gatherings revolved around the person being pushed to confess by the priest, accompanied by drumming, singing, and dancing. All of this amplified social interaction to a high pitch marked by the point at which the fowl slain by the priest finally collapsed in a manner that satisfied the fetish. Then, as the reporter stated, "the release of tension came like a flood." This was high drama, not in the Greek tradition, but rather more akin to the Stanislauski "method" of acting in which audience as well as those in the center stage came away fulfilled.

The Ashanti fetish provokes a query as to why the "witches" it attracted received such mild treatment at the hands of the priest and audience, in comparison with the harsh and often terminal disposition of witches and sorcerers in other parts of Africa and in New Guinea. While intralineage conflict, hostilities, and guilt help explain the underlying aggression, it was directed at witchcraft rather than at witches *per se*.

The explanation for what may be termed a "negative case" in the social control of witchery most likely resides in the specifics of the situation, in a conjunction or synergism of the old and the new that satisfied the feeling needs of different groups. These included native women who were excluded from participation in Christian churches, young men deprived of their traditional warrior roles, and even educated natives who could feel pride in something different but essentially African.

Whether cultures are disrupted by migration or by the inroads of colonialism, a collective hiatus of meaning is likely to emerge that is best filled by cult beliefs and rituals close to the exigencies of daily life. Ward (p. 66) presents the matter as follows:

> It may be that the universalistic religions, with their single all-powerful but seemingly remote deities, often seem incapable of meeting the requirements of individuals who feel themselves in need of reassurance in the happenings of everyday life. So old rituals are retained, or where they are not suited to the new situations, new ones are evolved. But such new developments can never be entirely without local precedent.[3]

---

3. This conclusion is remarkably similar to that reached about the popular culture of evil in urban South India. See Caplan, Lionel, in the *Anthropology of Evil*, ch. 7.

5

Evil and Social Control
in Melanesia

Piecing out the account or story or the sociocultural picture
of evil and social control takes on a more lurid cast when its
provenience is Melanesia *vis a vis* Africa. By this I refer not only
to the exotic physical appearance of its native inhabitants but
also to their early proclivities for eating human flesh, their endemic wars and feuding, their gross gender conflict and, paradoxi-
cally, their sensitivity to shame. Beyond these features one
encounters the great diversity of Melanesian cultures and the difficulties of fitting their social organization into accepted anthropological descriptive categories. The task of sorting out and
comparing social control and law in the "crazy quilt" of Melanesian cultures is one calculated to restore the medieval virtue
of humility to the brashest of scholars (Lawrence, 1987, pp. 15ff.).

Ethnographers working their claims in Melanesia proved to
be a different lot from their African confreres, distinguished from
the anthropological theory of the time by the attention given
to psychological factors. Fortune, for example, who came into
anthropology from psychology, stated that he "hoped to find a
middle ground which would illuminate the character of a
people" (1932, p. xi).

The fact that sorcery rather than witchcraft predominated
in Melanesia has given more empirical substance to the study
of occult beliefs and associated practices there. By this I mean
that in contrast to the phantasy nature of witches, there were
flesh and blood persons—local residents, mostly male—who
were known and identifiable as sorcerers. Moreover they used

known materials and specifiable rites for their purposes, provided services for payment and in some cases sought to cure
sickness.[1]

However, it must be added that there were Melanesian
societies in which people at times argued and debated the
problem of sorcery vociferously without any evidence coming
to light that anyone actually did anything to justify their fears
in the matter (Bowden, 1987, p. 184). This parallels Selby's (1974)
finding for the Zapotecs, namely that although his villagers
believed in witches, no evidence existed that anyone ever practiced rituals or cast spells (supra, 62).

One can conclude with reasonable assurance that a popular
culture of evil flourished among Melanesian peoples in the sense
that ordinary persons had access to sorcery arts, either learned
from one's father or available through hiring a known sorcerer.
Some common forms of sorcery reputedly worked through
poisons introduced into the food of victims, incantations over
their "leavings," and by magical attacks with slivers shot into
the victim's body. Finally to be noted is that, in some areas at
least, natives knew how to apply magic to stimulate growth in
their gardens and to protect them from intruders or thieves.

The Issue of Evil

The designation of sorcery as evil appears to have been less distinctive for Melanesian peoples than held true for African societies.
Whether or not sorcery qualified as evil depended on motives for
its use, the forms and directions it took, the persons or forces who
activated it, plus the fear and revulsion associated with it in
time and space. Generally speaking, the native conviction that
sorcery served as a means for social control of deviant and socially
unacceptable behavior, along with its conservative influences
and popular accessibility, lent it socially redeeming value despite
its close connection with disease, misfortune, and death.

Melanesians of New Britain are said to have made this
explicit (Chowning, 1974, p. 194):

---

1. For Systematic statement of the differences between the sorcerer and the witch
see Stephen, 1987, pp. 265–279.

the practice of sorcery is not considered criminal in itself. Men freely admit to being sorcerers, and the adherence of many young men to ancestral ways is a result of their fear of sorcery at the hands of older men.

The author of this comment stated that she encountered only one man who believed that sorcery was an evil in itself and that Christianity most certainly had influenced his ideas.

Hogbin (1947, p. 281) attributed the pragmatic attitude towards sorcery to the situational morality of the native people he studied, citing words of a missionary who lived among the Busama: "They have no moral principles still less moral laws. They have the notion of the forbidden and permitted but not of good and evil." Yet he also stated that the performance of magic within the village is considered evil (p. 282). The qualified view of sorcery and warfare as "necessary evils" was described by an older member of the Suolol society in the New Guinea Highlands, who recalled the suffering, death, and disruption it caused, but at the same time stated that it was necessary to establish equivalence and balance in society (Lederman, 1981, p. 19). In summing up Melanesian morality, Stephen (1987, p. 271) echoed Hogbin's conclusion that it was defined in specific situations—a product of action, not moral principle.

This overstates the case if the conclusion is that Melanesians had no conception of evil or that they were completely amoral. The very idea of "necessary evil" refutes such a notion. Furthermore the absence of discernible moral principles does not exclude the experiencing of evil as something apart from or over and beyond simple good/bad moral feelings. Nor does ascription of an apparent relative morality to a people recognize its cosmological implications, which admit sources of evil other than sorcery.

Reay (1987, p. 87) makes explicit reference to evil inadvertently brought into clan territory by visitors, evil bush spirits, spirits of the dead, and angry ghosts. These references necessarily move thought more generally to the influence of deities and spirits, ancestral or otherwise, in some kind of overriding moral judgments not only of problematic good/bad actions of human beings but also of their control or punishment of sorcery.

Malinowski in his early work found a well developed conception of evil and "evil magicians" among the Mailu (1988, pp. 170–175). These people expressed in words and behavior their intense dread of night as the time when a man made invisible, a *bardu*, ranged widely, being said to enter dwellings where he killed and revived men, also pausing to copulate with sleeping women, all very reminiscent of the *incubi*, said to roam the night in Gothic Europe.

Sorcery Fear

One measure of evil may be the fear that sorcery strikes in those at risk as potential victims. Whether this was comparable to that of witch fear described for African societies is a contestable question. Fortune (1932, p. 137) painted the darkest picture of sorcery, indicating that the ubiquitous suspicion and distrust it caused was characteristic of the Dobuan Islanders:

> the whole life of the people is strongly colored by a thorough absence of trust in neighbors and the practice of treachery beneath a show of friendliness. Every person goes in fear of the secret war and on frequent occasions the fear breaks through to the surface. Fortune attributed this pervasive air of threat to the exceptionally heterogeneous population in Dobu, which was produced by marriage and divorce practices.

However, Todd (1935, p. 431) challenged the idea that Melanesians of this period lived in constant fear of sorcery, claiming rather that such fear was latent and came into play for New Britain natives only in extreme situations—to which I add, much as it did among the Yokuts-Mono people of California.[2]

---

2. Kimball Young once proposed to a class at Harvard University where I served as his reader that Fortune's personal feelings of paranoia may have distorted his findings about the Dobuans. Fortune himself (1932, p. 160) referred to his "rough and ready" field methods, the use of cajolery, and of threats to coerce informants. On one occasion at a conference in Ohio, Fortune confided over drinks that he once shot a native for throwing a dead cat into his water hole. While I found Fortune's writing style strange in places, his description and analysis impressed me as being internally consistent and generally in line with other studies in the area of his research.

The "bad" and "necessary evil" aspects of sorcery came from recognition that antisocial behavior, quarrels, and sorcery all go hand-in-hand, and that failure to meet kinship obligations, stealing, and adultery cause "bad feelings." For the natives of New Britain, deaths attributed to sorcery interfered with the cycle of mortuary observances and put an end to feasts and dances. In these aspects sorcery became evil by implication, depending on the extent to which bad feelings were exacerbated or became transcendent.

Crises and Evil

Sorcery where it existed was part of the problems of everyday existence for Melanesians living in close, face-to-face relationships; it was acceped as unavoidable or necessary, in some cases even by its victims or their kin. At its best it led to negotiation, settled differences, dealt with deviants, and allowed life to go on one way or another. Its ambiguous, good/evil aspects made it bearable as a means of social control, rough and uncertain though it was.

Such acceptance reflected or made for a kind of social equilibrium. This, however, could give way to crises, depending on changes due to epidemics of sickness, increase of deaths, or other intrusive factors. When contingencies created by crises affected large numbers of people and threatened their survival or their way of life, their conception of sorcery lost its ambiguity to become a foreboding presence of unqualified evil. Such, for example, proved to be true of the Fore people living in the Eastern Highlands of Papua.

An incursion of slow acting, debilitating virus disease, *Kuru*, began in the second quarter of the present century. At its peak the virus caused two hundred deaths per year; by 1957 it had killed twenty-five hundred people, mostly women in their child-bearing years. This also struck directly at male prerogatives, not only leaving them without wives but also the labor necessary to cultivate gardens and tend pigs whence came their food supply (Lindenbaum, 1979, p. 6).

While outside research revealed *Kuru* to be caused by cannibalizing bodies of the dead, Fore men laid it to "evil practices" of sorcerers, whom they called to come forth and confess at public gatherings termed *Kibungo,* somewhat in the manner of Quaker meetings. In net effect the Fore recognized the "hidden warfare" of factionalism and the resultant sorcery as a "crime against society." In the course of meetings the Fore pictured their sorcerers as being compulsively driven by their special food and drink to "maintain the hot effects of their evil work" (p. 122). This self-deprecation was verified by visitors from a neighboring tribe, who referred to the Fore as "evil people always working at sorcery."

Speeches at the *Kibungo* clearly raised moral issues of adherence to the new ways of white men and "old ways" of the Fore. Public confessions of guilt emphasized the "moral discomfort" felt by a group confronted with a "breach of the natural order" (Turner, 1957) such as that experienced by the Fore.

Seen in times of crisis, native morality emerges or is created anew from some perceived natural order, one in which values and value ordering take explicit shape. This is not unlike the process presented by W. G. Sumner many years ago (1906) in which unconsciously held group habits, or folkways, are converted by crises into mores, made socially compelling by ethical generalizations as to why their observance is necessary for group welfare.

Hamilton's writings, also of older vintage (1932), describe a similar process in which the institutions of modern society, ordinarily taken for granted, in parlous times are brought to the surface of thought and feeling by clarification of their nature. In a prophetic way—at least for my analysis here—he held this process equally applicable to: "The folk of the South Seas islands . . . [who] can neither give answers to hypothetical cases nor tell in the abstract what they do" (p. 88).

From this line of thought it is apparent that the idea of a purely situated morality of the native peoples of Melanesia needs amendment to account for their episodic, raised awareness of deep-lying, taken-for-granted values that in group interaction reshaped their overt behavior. In the presented case this led to the decision to abandon and ritually repudiate *Kuru* type sorcery and to reestablish older group bonds that had been eroded by dissension and conflict (Lindenbaum, 1979, pp. 65ff.).

Evil and Resolution of Ambiguity

What has been written here about the Fore leads to a conclusion that situations may arise in the history of a society sufficiently critical or apocalyptic in nature to reveal or lead to the creation of an overarching morality in which the ambiguities of good and evil are at least temporarily reconciled. One hesitates to say that the depradations of *kuru* "put the fear of God" in the Fore people, but it may have changed their perspective sufficiently to admit cosmological considerations as to the source of their plight. Indeed it is possible that more searching ethnographic inquiries might disclose beliefs or implicit values of a relatively fixed nature that influence native thought, interaction, and choice. In different terms, it may be pragmatic in some situations to think in nonpragmatic ways, particularly if one's way of life faces extinction.

The Righteous Gebusi

Evidence that awareness of something like cultural themes, ethos, or patterned values unequivocally condemning sorcery as evil was not entirely alien to Melanesian societies is at hand in accounts of Gebusi intransigence in the matter. Gebusi searched out sorcerers through spirit seances that did not just establish a sorcerer's identity and guilt but actively conveyed an "overwhelming sense of moral righteousness and collective legitimacy of their attributions." In the words of Knauft (1985, p. 310) "there is no moral ambiguity but only virtuous retribution against those who have proven themselves irredeemably evil." The seances in question here had something in common with those conducted by Azande medicine men (supra, 54) but went far beyond their tentative, indirect, and implied revelations. The Gebusi seance in all cases presented sorcery as total evil, contrary to their ethos or morality of the community. The intensity or forcefulness of the spiritual condemnations were reflected in instances in which kin of the victim openly opposed actions to execute one of their own as a sorcerer. The exceptionally high rate of homicides by the Gebusi, including those for sorcery, further attested to their obduracy in dealing with sorcery. It may be that the depth of emotion felt when basic patterned values of a people are dramatically threatened, in this context by sorcery, does much to account for their collective experience of evil. The store the Gebusi set on "good company" with their special emphasis on amity, plus their manneristic denial of hostility and anger by social withdrawal and compulsive "yelling," speak to a kind of fomented cultural or collective transcendence conducive to the experience of evil, however specious it may have seemed (Knauft, 1985, ch. 11). A somewhat similar emotional intensity characterized the attitudes and reactions of the Tangu people living on the North Coast of New Guinea, whose paramount values were those of amity, equivalence, and moral equality, values continually reaffirmed and reiterated during assemblies. The sense of the moral for the Tangu lay in reciprocity (Burridge, 1965, pp. 227ff.):

They have no authority. Equivalence, expressed in prestation, is the radical note of being in the moral order.

Evil for the Tangu was personified by the nonreciprocal man, a *ranguma*, who in their cosmology was the last man to come out of a hole into the world. The word translates variously as "sorcerer," "criminal," "assassin," "scapegoat" and "nonconformist." More precisely, *ranguma* refers to an uncontrollable one, who may use sorcery to cause sickness that keeps others away from garden work, whose produce is necessary to fulfill their reciprocal obligations within the village scheme of life. Suspected of sorcery, the *ranguma* was forced to confess, have his gardens trashed, and compelled to pay compensation.

Beliefs and punitive actions revolving around the *ranguma* strike one as midway between those about witches and those applicable to sorcerers. While sorcerers were persons who succumbed to temptation to misuse power, *ranguma* were believed to be without inner control. Yet, unless they were outsiders, they could be reintegrated within the community—an unusual example of liberal social control for Melanesians in its approximation of the modern idea of rehabilitation.

All of this suggests that some Melanesian peoples, at least, did have explicitly structured value orders in regard to the evils of sorcery. These were continuously active rather than latent influences on social control and did not require crises to activate them. This turns attention to the importance of ethos, themes, or patterns of culture as factors in the complete understanding of societal reactions to evil. More precisely it raises for consideration the ways in which major cleavages in cultures or dialectical value systems influence social control.

Melanesian Witchcraft as Unmitigated Evil

Witchcraft, conceived as intrinsic or inherited power exercised through spells, "at a distance" is of lesser importance than sorcery in the Melanesian cultural panorama, being confined to relatively few areas and tribes, and whose attendant beliefs and practices could well have been imported. Stephen (1987, p. 263) however, stated that recognition of witches may be more common than ordinarily believed, and he listed fourteen tribes in which this was true. Generally, with minor exceptions, women were identified with or accused of witchery (Patterson, 1974, p. 145).

Depictions of the Melanesian witches resemble those of their counterparts in African societies, in some cases fully matching their repulsive character. This prompted Stephen (1987, p. 262) to speak of the "the classic image of the witch . . . a creature of inhuman appetites and sheer evil." Kalam witch beliefs revolved around notions of power, or *koyb*, emanating from a snakelike creature that, having invaded the stomach of a human being, enabled her to assume animal form, become invisible, move swiftly from place to place, and kill at a distance. The image of the witch was "a caricature of uncontrolled female substances: fat, dull, nasty, covered with grease, sweat, heat, pollution and black blood—all exudations from massive, deformed genitalia" (Poole, 1981, p. 64; Stephen, 1987, p. 276).

Interaction of Witch Suspects and Others

The horrific ideology of Melanesian witches, in common with those of Africa, served to dehumanize those accused and provide a rationale for their rejection as well as for ridding a group of their presence by ejection from the community or execution. Melanesian witch data in common with those of Africa draw attention to a class of stereotyped persons who were marginal participants in social activity. They were distinguished by their appearance but also by the behavior associated with their social isolation: solitary walks, eating voraciously, failure to share food, neglect of attire, and in the company of dogs or cats.

Reay (1987, p. 93) wrote of changes in the behavior of presumed witches resulting from their isolation: "They were beginning to reject the sociable, extroverted and energetic Kuma life style. Lethargy, gloomy disposition, carelessness of dress, chronic absent-mindedness and breaches of social conventions marked them off from others." All of this fits very well a process pattern of secondary deviance, as the suspected or accused was "forced to exhibit a sorcery habit," and "aware that he is being treated as a witch, he may well wonder if he is one" (p. 6).

Scapegoat Theory and the Emergence of Evil

An easy conclusion from the above may be that Melanesians singled out persons to accuse of witchcraft from among a stigmatized or powerless class: old persons, rubbish men, eccentrics, or behavioral deviants who ignored the expectations and dominant values of the community. However, this notion does not mesh well with the apparent fact that in-married women were regarded with suspicion in many Melanesian societies, as well as children in some cases, and men who could not be classed as failures. Moreover some of those thought to be witches might be members of a clan whose members as a whole had sufficient and clear motives for "casting down the mighty," to use Fortune's felicitous phrase. From this vantage, interclan rivalry or "politics" reveals more about witchcraft accusations than reference to traits of individuals. Considerations such as these, among others, led Reay (1987, p. 113) to conclude that it was difficult to say that Kuma witches were or were not scapegoats.[3]

---

3. Kluckhohn makes this same point when he says that the scapegoat function is "not a sufficient explanation for specific forms of Navaho witchcraft" (Kluckhohn, 1944, pp. 90, 97).

Successful stigmatizing of suspects as witches may better be seen as a product of group interaction that creates new meanings of behavior and the particularistic assessment of personality traits rather than as a simple matching of the latter to a local stereotype of evildoers. The plausibility of specific accusations and the vulnerability of an individual rather than status *per se* became critical factors in such interaction. In this light, Hewa women got targeted for witchcraft accusations in part because others believed that they invisibly cannibalized people, but also because, being deprived of protein, they had good reason to do so (Steadman, 1975, p. 118). A final point is that in-married Hewa women were vulnerable to accusations because they had no ready partisans to come to their support.

Even when those accused of witchcraft bore stigma, their other characteristics could be atypical, such as their gender. Motivation for their extinction might inhere in the problems their groups experienced with other groups. Reay (1976) documented some of the atypicalities and complexities of a witch hearing in which those executed were males rather than females. Both victims and those seeking their demise belonged to the same subclan, which was declining in numbers and was impoverished. Those promoting what was much like a "witch cleansing" looked to receive material aid (pigs, fowl and pork) in return for their nefarious work, in which one of the accused accused another, and the latter in turn accused a third person and thus "shifted the blame in a deadly ritual" (Reay, 1976, p. 8). All of the men were executed merely on their confessions and the word of others, apparently without any other evidence of malfeasance. Whatever purpose the political machinations served, they proved to be counterproductive in a larger sense because the size of their "fewgroup" diminished further.

Unsettled Issues

One of the unsettled issues in ethnographic treatments of Melanesian-style sorcery concerns the group affiliations of the sorcerer and his victim. One point of view holds that sorcerers directed their malice towards persons identified with an enemy people or an outgroup. Hogbin's (supra, 95) early informant indicated that this was true for the Busama by stating that "the performance of magic within the village is considered evil." In the same vein Berndt (1962, p. 211) asserted that "sorcery within the district between its members-so-called endo sorcery, was strongly condemned." Whether such observations reflected actual behavior is debatable, particularly since sorcery was practiced secretly and in times of personal crisis.

The facts of warfare sorcery on the surface support the idea that its users sought victims among an outgroup, and for some tribes this was the only kind of sorcery practiced. However, warfare sorcery is difficult to reconcile with the basic ideas about the roots of sorcery, which reside strongly in emotions in close-bonded relationships. Hence warfare sorcery is in an important sense anomalous in that it lacks the close interpersonal element and is openly carried out and with the approval of the group at war. Such sorcery has the look of generalized magic similar to that employed to protect gardens and pigs.

Reay (1987, p. 91) refers to "A" sorcerers who directed their arts against a few men in the enemy clan who were personally known to them, namely fight leaders and opposing "A" sorcerers. However, there is no mention of interpersonal conflicts between the targeted individuals and those making the sorcery. This suggests that such targets were selected for strategic or tactical reasons.

A study by Sillitoe (1978) revealed indirectly that political groups warring to redress wrongs, such as theft, sex offenses, payment failures, and property offenses, lived in close proximity, exchanged women for marriage, and intermittently ceased warfare to carry on trade, feasts, and ceremonies. In contrast, those political groups engaged in unceasing warfare fought for individual prestige and because "to fight is right"; they had no close ties for trade or ceremonies and no marriages with enemy women. Sorcery was a reason given for groups seeking redress in seventy percent of their wars, but only fourteen percent for groups habitually or culturally given to war-making. While the data in this study are only loosely coupled, they suggest some significant differences on the part of the culturally militant groups in making choices between warfare and sorcery as a means to express aggression.

While it is no doubt true that Melanesians living continuously in close proximity were likely to avoid making sorcery
among themselves, nevertheless a nearby "on-again off-again
enemy" known, for example, to the Abelam people, made a
particular kind of ingroup sorcery possible. This was facilitated
by reason of the individual ties and marriages with outgroup
women. A man so married asked his wife to make sorcery
against one in his own group for whom he bore malice. This
was risky for if discovered the wife might become the object
of attack.

A more complicated way to sorcerize an ingroup member
involved connivance between (1) a sorcerer in an enemy village,
(2) a supplier of "leavings," usually someone within the victim's
village, and (3) a person who pays to have the evil deed done
(Forge, 1970, p. 263). Number two person usually was someone
who had valid reason for movement between the two villages,
usually the wife of number three, originally from the enemy
village. Big men also might become party to plots with something like blackmarket trading in sorcery materials.

A methodological question arises at this juncture as to the
validity of efforts of ethnographers of Melanesian sorcery and
witchcraft to specify their directionality or disapproval according
to the groups categorized by the conventional discourse of
anthropology: agnatic, lineal, clan and subclan, parish, and
village. The movements of individuals between Melanesian
population concentrations and their resultant heterogeneity
leave it unclear that affiliations for specific social action were
in fact identifiable by such categories. In some instances villages
contained both agnates and nonagnates, including matrilineal
kin, refugees, and visitors with weak or fictive ties to the locality.
Those in agnate groups frequently were unable to trace their
ancestry and moreover not interested in doing so.

Attenuated identities were most obvious for married women
of Melanesia, who, as with exogamous societies or groups, were
neither acting members of their natal group nor fully accepted
members of their husband's. However, this also applied to men;
thus where a man slept might tell nothing about his social
bonding to obtain and cultivate garden land. While the implications of marginal status for married women in relation to

conspiratorial ingroup sorcery have been described by ethnographers (Fortune, 1932; Berndt, 1962), those deriving from the fact that men may identify and act with different groups either at enmity or amity with one another have not (Barnes, 1962). The extent to which this is true is hard to say, but it makes more understandable reports that intracommunity sorcery is very much a part of the social life of a number of Melanesian societies (Chowning, 1987, p. 171; Bowden, 1987, pp. 193–199).

However useful structural concepts have been for ethnographic studies, other kinds of descriptive terms may be necessary to comprehend sorcery and witchcraft of Melanesian societies, characterized as they have been by the dynamics of continual warfare and feuding. Such terms also are very much needed to enlighten the difficulties of social control resulting from population movements and multiple membership in parish groups.[4]

General Aspects of Social Control in Melanesia

One can safely generalize that, with the possible exception of warfare, most social control in Melanesian societies was primarily and even essentially interpersonal in nature, the action of one person trying to compel another to comply with his/her demands, or to seek redress for harm done.

Lawrence (1966), in writing about the Gahuka Gama, classified their social controls under three headings: (1) self-regulation resulting from childhood and ongoing socialization, (2) reciprocities, and (3) sanctions. Reciprocities resulted from satisfactions of values or "goods." For example, "it is good to distribute pork," clear the bush for gardens, help build homes, and attend funerals. Such moral obligations arose from self-interest or the need for survival. They held only within the clan, for the same patrilineage, patriclan and subclan (p. 33). Taken together these values, when satisfied, reflect passive social control or are an integral part of it.

---

4. Huli people, among whom "residential fluidity is the rule," exemplify a kind of anarchy or individualism which made social control difficult even within kinship groups (Glasse, 1965, p. 48).

Sanctions for a delict like theft consisted of preventive magic or, if the thief was known, a demand for compensation. Killing domestic pigs prompted retaliation from their owner, either by killing pigs of the thief or insistence on compensation. Adultery stirred the husband to violence, sorcery, or again, a demand for compensation. In cases of homicide, relatives took revenge by violence or sorcery. Marriage within the consanguine group provoked strong measures of violence or sorcery plus annulment of the marriage. Generally speaking the closer the relationship of the offender and the person wronged and the fewer the people involved, the less severe was the retaliation and the easier it was to reach a settlement (Lawrence, 1966, p. 32).

Assemblies called to consider social troubles generally attracted kinsmen of the parties rather than an entire village population. There was no fixed authority at such meetings. "Big Men" or "Elders" could encourage or influence agreements, but they had no judicial power. Nor did assemblies necessarily reach a consensus about disputes or responsibility for offenses. The "sense of the meeting," if there was one, tended to emerge later, implicit in the actions of those with an interest in the dispute or deviance. Oddly, no reference was made to the use of shame or shaming as a means of control for the Gahuka-Gama, perhaps because the author was writing a report that could be used by law makers.

Shame and Social Control:
A Melanesian Paradox

The influence of values and their cultural patterning on social control among Melanesians is not easily sorted out. Epstein (1984) wrote of patterns of social control in his work on shame in Melanesian cultures, but he did not pursue their nature. What can be said is that importance of sanctions and their use varied greatly in New Guinea and Papua. Sorcery, for example, while widespread, was relatively unimportant or even believed to be undesirable by some Melanesian people. While witchcraft could be found in some societies, sorcery occurred much more frequently.

An exception to variable nature of the use of particular social controls in Melanesia lay in the effects of shame, which Langness

(1965) held to be a powerful emotion and a "universal notion among the peoples of Papua and New Guinea." Beyond this statement one meets with problems of understanding and analysis in that shame emerges in a great variety of cultural contexts. The term is not easily defined nor translatable from the words natives apply to it. Hence, ethnographers must make do with connotations rather than the denotations of shame phenomena.

Like the difficulty early ethnographers had in understanding and conveying the idea that Africans believed that witches killed people, those at work in New Guinea had to try to find explanations for a paradox, namely that Melanesians, who practiced sorcery, waged ruthless wars of revenge including the wanton killing of women and children, but nevertheless were highly sensitive to their internal feelings of shame.

Of course, shaming and shame are known as a means of social control in other societies of the world, including the Puritan colonies of America, where criminals were branded and exposed in stocks to public gaze, and where authorities compelled adulterous women to wear a scarlet "A" sewn on their dresses. Native Americans, ferocious in war, are said to have lost all aplomb when subjected to ridicule. The difference for Melanesians lay in the extent to which shame and shaming serve as a deterrent and sanction and its complex relationships with nudity; sexual intercourse; defecation; and, above all, with the growing, exchange, and consumption of food.[5]

That which caps the paradox of Melanesian sensitivity to shame was the outlandish manner in which the natives sought to shame others. To the Western way of thinking it reverses the expectation that a person taking offense will strike back or oppose the offender in some way. Instead the nettled native

---

5. Michael Young in his study of *Fighting With Food* (1976) has richly documented the cultural importance of food so conspicuous in Melanesia. From shreds of evidence encountered in my studies of alcohol use in Polynesia I suggest that the cultural salience of food is widespread throughout Oceania. Certainly it held true for status distinctions in Hawaii. In the 1960s when I sat at huge meals with Samoans they wondered if I were sick despite my 170 pounds. Tahitians spoke of me with concern as being *maigre*. Finally, one may find amusement in William Lessa's do-it-yourself TAT test that clearly showed Ulithians much more interested in food than sex.

among those tribes in which it is reported, sought redress by self-injury or self-castigation by such means as refusing all food, giving his food products to others, running away from one's home, giving one's self up to the enemy, destroying one's dwelling or the produce in his gardens, suicide by hanging in a tree, or, as in the well known case described by Malinowski, leaping to one's death from a palm tree.

Shame as Passive Social Control

Shame refers to a special set of feelings with both subjective and objective aspects. Subjectively shame is associated with concealed shortcomings of individuals, their weaknesses, foibles, and past deviance, as well as behavior and thoughts culturally defined as private. The affect of shame, described by Melanesians, is in part physiological, being "on the skin," or in a "hot belly," or "on the brow." Shame feelings are similar to those provoked by overgazing, demonstrable by simply pointing a finger at a student by a class instructor without comment. Psychologically, shame is felt as ephemeral self-loathing associated with failure to keep intact the individual's virtual identity (Goffman's term, 1963)

Parenthetically one may wonder whether Melanesian feelings of shame are part of the experience of evil, bringing to mind the Fore picture of sorcerers, who ate special food to sustain the "hot effects of their evil work" (supra, 97). Larger speculation suggests that experiencing incongruent, "out of place" heat may connote evil for Melanesians as well as for Euro-Americans imbued with images of Dante's Inferno and fires of hell stoked by the devil.[6]

From a passive control perspective the anticipation of shame acted as a powerful deterrent, particularly if the person feared being found out. Hence it typically applied to premeditated or malicious disregard of the reciprocal expectations of others. The binding quality of reciprocities, referred to as *maya* by one of Hogbin's (1947, p. 287) informants, was phrased as follows: "it

---

6. For further discussion of the relation of heat to sorcery see Fortune, R., 1932, appendix IV, Heat and the Black Art.

holds us fast like an anchor stone mooring a canoe." Thus the Busamo complied with expectations, such as avoiding divorce of a barren wife, helping others construct gardens, and paying more for craft items than their market value because to do otherwise would cause people to talk about them. Above all, so Hogbin (p. 274) tells us, "no Busamo would sink so low as to ask others for food."

Sanctions

It is common knowledge that internal "self-control" motivated by anticipated consequences does not work very well when the powerful drives of sex or anger are at work. Sexual dalliance leading to adultery, for example, ordinarily grows out of fortuitous contacts, without forethought, in which immediate pleasure suppresses the anticipated risks of discovery. Beyond this, in the Melanesian instances, the anger of a physically abused wife or one sexually dissatisfied with her older husband gave reason to run away with another man. In such instances the husband might respond by subjecting the wife to public rape (Berndt, 1962, ch. 9). Otherwise he might physically attack the man, sorcerize him, or confront him by means of the *abutu*, a competitive food exchange.

Sanctions for Melanesians as well as for those in other societies often were more expressive or symbolic than regulative in nature. So, for example, while the cuckolded Kalauna husband might feel better at having bested his wife's seducer in the *abutu*, it did not necessarily bring his wife back. Young (1974, p. 223) concluded that the effect of the outcome of the intragroup *abutu* was largely symbolic in that it revealed the disapproval of the community whose partisans pro and con took part in the accumulation and distribution of food. Larger cultural values came to the fore and a moral dimension was given to the conflict, in the course of which competing groups ultimately reached a kind of detente.

As this kind of interpretation indicates, saying that social control among Melanesians takes the form of self-help may overlook the organizational ramifications of interpersonal conflict and the clan or district interests which influence the ultimate effects of attempted social control. The possibility exists, although I have not found direct ethnographic evidence for it, that an individual may be well aware of such facts and may have been playing a kind of primitive politics by self-deprivation and self-punishment.

Such "politics" can be played even when the stakes are very high, such as the risk or probability of death. The case of Kimai, described by Malinowski, of a Trobriander man denounced by a frustrated suitor for committing technical incest, that of outside the immediate family, with his former lover illustrates the point here.

Kimai climbed a palm tree, explained that he was going to kill himself and blamed the jilted lover for his act, then leaped sixty feet to his death. While Malinowski stated that the man acted as his own executioner, it was clear that his act aimed to rouse hostility towards his accuser, which succeeded when his clan brothers attacked and beat him, then repeated the attack the next day at the funeral (Hoebel, 1968, pp. 183ff.).[7]

Shaming

The sensitivity of Melanesians to shaming in relation to deterrence or self-control undoubtedly is connected in part with their early socialization. Thus Busamo mothers constantly urged their children of early years to keep their genitals covered and to avoid stealing (especially food) and open sex behavior. At the same time these children learned not to embarrass others by talking about their misdeeds. This sounds a little like the conspiracy of silence about sex in Victorian England. However, the silence on sex was a derived one, and it would be incorrect to regard Melanesians as sexually repressed. Rather the anxiety about sex derived from the anxiety about food production, for a man and wife found copulating in the bush or in their garden

---

7. Raymond Firth interpreted suicide in Tikopia as a form of risk-taking rather than a Durkheimian response to anomie, a concept few would apply to Polynesians. Such an act brought covert conflict to light and redefined it socially. The difference between attempted suicide and actual suicide merely depended on the degree of risk involved and chance factors, such as whether the suicidal persons swam beyond the reef of the lagoon or returned from solitary voyages out to sea.

would mark them as *dilettantes*, by their behavior denying the salient importance of growing food.

Sensitivity to shame was not uniformly inculcated and it varied from person to person. Those deprived of "normal" socialization due to having no caring parents apparently proved to be unresponsive to shaming. Women were said to be less sensitive than men on the matter and, finally, Big Men, by reason of their more aggressive nature and their special social roles, were less vulnerable to shaming than others.

Sensitivity to shaming, as already noted, went beyond the individual to groups with which persons identified. According to Williams' (1930) findings on the Orakavia of an early period, the feeling of *Meh*, that of shame, humiliation, and contrition, was "no more than fear of injuring the feelings of the 'sympathy group.' " It is here that the importance of the clan and/or the sympathy group, came to bear; so the intraclan offender did not get off scot free, as sometimes implied (Moore, 1965; supra, 79; Oberg, 1934) even though the victim does not strike back, but injures himself in some way. For the Orakavia "the offender could not stand to see pain or feel anger of the man wronged when occurring within the sympathy group" (Williams, 1930, p. 330). These emotions became the transmuted feelings of close-bonded clan others, which were "no less effective than the fear of retaliation or fear of reprobation in keeping the individual from doing wrong" (p. 534). Likewise, "if a man commits an unjustifiable offense, not only does the victim suffer, but the culprit's fellows, who feel that they share his responsibility, will be positively covered with vicarious *Meh*" (p. 321).

Williams mentions that powerful warriors sometimes engaged in tyrannical behavior and became a terror to the neighborhood, but gave no indication of how others dealt with them (p. 319). One possibility is suggested by Hoebel's (1968) observation that when Trobriander chiefs in league with sorcerers became tyrannical, individuals subjected to their coercive actions struck back with sorcery of their own (pp. 187ff.). The barebones nature of the available data on this subject makes it difficult to say whether shaming was an applicable social control in instances where differences in power existed. The least to be said is that Big Men, as already noted, were less vulnerable to shame than others. Yet they were not immune to its effects. Reay (1953, p. 110) referred to an Orakavia case in which a cuckolded husband did not confront the man involved but rather relied on a "bonded friend" to call him disparaging names. What this means is unclear. Williams (1930, p. 327) stated that sorcery was available to the weak and strong alike for purposes of retaliation. Whether this was comparable to the practice of the Comanche people of allowing a "champion" to confront a more powerful aggressor is difficult to say.

The Strange Case of the Toltai Remedies

An apparent exception to the importance of shame as a social contol in Melanesian societies comes from early accounts of the Toltai people. That by Kleintitschen (1906), cited by Sack (1974, pp. 67–68), left the impression that brute force or the payment of shell money allowed powerful and dominant men to "get away with anything," including incest. Nevertheless a Toltai morality condemned rape, sexual promiscuity, lying, and theft (p. 82). It had to be implemented by self-help whereby a victim seeking to remedy a wrong sought the aid of others, i.e., "to get them on his side" by one means or another. This could mean that a sexually promiscuous woman so shamed her relatives that they wounded or killed her. Relatives also took action against one of their own who committed incest, first decorating then killing him (p. 84).

However, the form of control changed when an individual was put at a disadvantage by the wrongful act of a more powerful man. One recourse in such situations was to engage a sorcerer and strike back. A victim of this sort also could get help from a secret Duk-Duk society. A much more dramatic tactic—a strangely perverse recourse against the powerful—was a kind of fighting fire with fire, the *kamara*. The victim in such cases committed a wrong similar to his own, against another "innocent" person; this person then repeated the act, until enough people had the power necessary to attack the original wrongdoer. Together they damaged gardens, cut down fruit trees, destroyed canoes, and set fire to dwellings.

To quote Sack (1974) on the matter:

In cases of adultery [so far as public courses of action
for the deceived husband against the adulterer (and his
group) are concerned] he could kill the man on the spot;
he could fight the adulterer [and his group] with the
support of his group or hired mercenaries, or with forced
allies; he could injure an innocent person, who would
then take revenge for him; he could demand compensation; he and his group could destoy property belonging
to the adulterer [or his group] to force compensation; he
could force public opinion by damaging property of
innocent people, into supporting his compensation
claim, or he could pay a chief to buy his compensation,
who would then collect it, plus a substantial interest.

It is not easy to make sense of the *kamara*, a point made
by Epstein (1974, p. 166), who believed that at best it applied
only to certain offenses or certain circumstances. The chain of
motivation involved in some of these remedies is bizarre, to say
the least.

While it could reflect some form of *ad hoc* theory of the
causation of wrongs held by the Toltai, more likely it was a way
of pyramiding avarice as a means of getting more compensation
for wrong, by multiplying the victims. Otherwise the account
has a stain of incredulity, somehow putting me in mind of
Charles Lamb's "Dissertation on Roast Pig."

Explanations of Shaming as Social Control

Attempts to explain the origin and development of shame
sanctions in Melanesia have not gone much beyond speculative
interpretations. One such speculation is that the absence of law
enforcement institutions gave rise to reliance on inducing shame
as a means of dispute resolution, readdressing grievances, and
restoring social order (Epstein, 1974). Young (1983, p. 263) speaks
more fully of this idea saying that the importance of shame in
Melanesian societies generally is likely related to their small
scale, their lack of formal juridical institutions, and their lateral

rather than hierarchical systems of authority—in short, to their egalitarian-based organization. Reay (1959) concluded that the "weak" social control system of the Orakaivans derived from the necessity of keeping aggression directed towards enemy groups. But one could argue that social control was weak in most Melanesian societies, which depended on self-help on which it rested; in the absence of authority individuals had to act, whether the control in question was violence, sorcery, or shaming.

Berndt (1962, p. 214) stated that victims of wrongs, or their relatives, did not always take revenge or seek redress when it was indicated. The people concerned (lineages) did not feel strongly about the matter, or chose to let things slide, or decided to leave revenge in the hands of the dead man's sons when they were grown, or they felt that the death balanced accounts with enemy groups. Inaction also could result from the lack of means to act or the inappropriateness of the sanction. Young (pp. 214ff.) tells of cases in which a wronged person did not have access to the necessary food supplies and pigs to stage an interpersonal type *abutu*. The implication that informal social controls, including shaming, occurring within lineages, agnate groups, or "sympathy groups" were weak, is an overbroad generalization. As Epstein (1974, p. 47) stated the matter, informal controls, including shaming, arose from interpersonal interaction in small societies, in which the values of equivalence and reciprocity predominated can be very powerful. The power is implicit in interpersonal interaction—in the use of words, avoidances, displays, dress, and ceremonial allusions—calculated to strike sensitive chords in others.

The Power of the Word

Undoubtedly words and symbolic actions took on a highly emotionalized meaning for many Melanesians due to a kind of conspiracy of silence about sensitive matters, particularly within informal groups. This left individuals vulnerable to exposure, coupled as it was with common knowledge about his/her status, such as whether a man owned the land where an argument arose, whether he had paid his bridal debts, the state of his obligations to his relatives, and what follies or deviance clouded his past. Children taught not to expose shortcomings of others— as with the Orakaivans—learned that reference to these could be a powerful tool for shaming when adults quarreled or became angry. Certain words or expressions apparently cut deep, as when two men quarreled in the presence of women. One might tell the other "go copulate with your wife," or conversely, a wife at odds with her husband could tell him to "go eat excrement" or "eat your mother's excrement." Todd (1936) reported that in the first instance cases occurred in which the man's wife hanged herself, and in the second instance the man divorced his wife. In still another case a widow, seeking to die in accordance with custom, asked her male relatives to kill her. When they refused she accused them of wanting to keep her to commit incest with her. Thus stung, they obliged her wish for death.

Shaming, as a form of symbolic interaction learned with the acquisition of self and identity, had some obvious advantages over other sanctions, such as fighting, sorcery or destoying one's property. Leaving aside the highly organized *abutu*, shaming had the advantage of immediacy; it emerged spontaneously, and "struck while the iron was hot." It required no preparation (in contrast to the *abutu*, or sorcery) since one could harangue another, give money from one's purse, or give a thief the pig he had already stolen. Shaming was less risky than violence and available to both sexes.

A final, perhaps clinching, note to make is that shaming provided an effective and appropriate means of guarding the jealously held values of equivalence threading through Melanesian cultures in that it dealt with the issue of power. The achieved power of the Big Man, like that of a Comanche warrior, had to be continuously reaffirmed, not only by exploits, but also by the opinions and actions of others. Todd (1936, p. 420) made this preeminently clear:

> The most effective curb on the authority of the headman and men of rank, is the fact that, like the most humble of their followers, they can be brought to shame and silence.

Public Opinion and Social Control

The subject of public opinion in relation to social control in Melanesian societies has not to my knowledge been treated as a topic in its own right. Rather its discussion has emerged as an aspect of dispute resolution, or as an influence on community-wide outcomes in validating or legitimating individual actions. Todd (1945, p. 440) was among the first if not the very first to speak on the matter, saying, "it has been the custom to speak of public opinion without, I think, clearly investigating whether this really exists." He further stated that action against one came because he had offended a large number of people. But unless a man is actively concerned about a dispute he has little interest in it and may avoid getting involved.

While this on its surface seems inconsistent with another of Todd's statements (supra, 127), that a Big Man could be shamed by a lower-ranking man, such shaming was interpersonal and structured by the situation. The extent to which such expressed opinions of Melanesians towards one another became community-wide or public in some classic democratic form, Western style, must remain problematic.

In contrast to Todd's skepticism about public opinion in Melanesian communities, Berndt (1962) almost thirty years later in his studies of New Guinea Highlands people, made numerous references—thirty-two in all—to public opinion as a form of social control, phrased as "social approval" of individual actions. Close examination revealed that Berndt's references to public opinion more or less presumed its existence, along with a tendency to reify the term, as a cause of other actions or as their result; e.g., "opinion is in favor of eating the corpse"; or, "interpersonal quarrels lead to a cleavages in opinion."

The one discussion of public opinion that Berndt treated as a separate topic had to do with meetings in the men's house, where opinion "was crystallized against the enemy" (p. 312). There the author made it clear that general discussion occurred but that it was largely controlled by local strong men, the warrior leaders, who were forceful speakers. This left little opportunity for other persons to express their views. Generally they were overridden by the more dominant men.

The Gahuka-Gama tribes recognized the right of any adult male to speak at gatherings; but this in effect meant anyone who was free of debt, who had repaid others for contributions to his initiation, and also had made his marriage payments. As Read (1959, p. 431) noted, "only a few were able to exercise this right."

Public Opinion and Social Organization

Undoubtedly all human beings in various ways express their opinions on controversial matters, Melanesians no less than others. Their influence, as shown in the above-noted strictures on expression, make it plain that the formation of public opinion depends to a great degree on the nature of the social organization or institutions through which it is voiced. Some years ago Walter Lippman's (1925) analysis gave the issue substance with his conclusion that public opinion in modern society was nothing more than the conflicts of particular interest groups that were projected into the public arena and not the expression of an omni-participating population.

Whether Lippman's conclusion applied to village or rural communities of the Anglo-Saxon tradition in Western societies may be questioned, so that the idea of some kind of inclusive or consensual social control in such settings cannot be rejected out of hand. Answers to the implied query both for Western and Melanesian communities must be sought in the forms of social organization and particular institutions through which opinions are articulated.

Certain kinds of rural and village institutions in early America undoubtedly provided special means, beginning with the emphasis on local education, for converting individual opinions into an operating consensus for community action. A facilitating factor was the availability of eighteenth-century political discourse for validating authority, accompanied by voting and majority rule birthed by social contract theories of Hobbes, Locke, and Rousseau and socially confirmed by an ideology of law (Davis, 1986). Even sectarian religious groups had ideologies and practices that validated authoritative decisions applicable to all—such as the Quaker "sense of the meeting," and the election day sermon of Calvanist ministers.

Ethnographers with Anglo-Saxon antecedents may have been overly concerned to discover evidence of a kind of public communication in Melanesian communities that actually may be unique to Western societies. In part this may have been due to confusion about the meaning of the term *public opinion*, which, as noted, has tended to be reified both in public usage and in scholarly writing. The confusion has its positive side in that the reification of public opinion, which reached an acme in Rosseau's conception of the *volonte generale*, and that of a corporate society help explain why democracies of the West could achieve, or at least socially validate, political authority, however unstable and uncertain its course of action or inaction has at times been.

Another possible source of confusion about the meaning of public opinion in Melanesian societies may lie in the term *equivalence* almost routinely employed to caption the basic values of Melanesian peoples. Superficially the term may be taken to mean "equality," but this is far from exact. Without some knowledge of its origin or original usage I turn to a distinction made by Hallpike (1977) who contrasted the social organization of an Ethiopian society with the Tauade of Melanesia, using the terms *Aristotelian* for the former and *Heroclitean* for the latter. For the first type society (preface, p. v):

> harmony will basically consist in the performance by members of each group and category of those tasks for which they are essentially fitted and qualified; thus 'right' will be distinct from 'power', and 'order' and 'truth' will be essential aspects of 'right.' The passions will be seen as destructive of the social order, and correspondingly one [finds] a basic concern with classification and conceptual boundaries . . .
>
> The opposite type of society . . . will be one that regards relationships between individuals as basic, and any existing groups as the precipitate of these relationships— friendship, enmity, revenge, and reciprocity in various forms, cooperation, marriages, competition and so on . . . 'harmony' will consist of the balance of opposing forces, and in this context will not be seen as destructive, but

on the contrary as providing the basis of all interaction, so the distinction between right and power becomes meaningless. Classification will have little relevance in such a system.

Actually Hallpike (p. 138ff.) seems to smoke up the ethnographer's glass when he rejects the ascriptive/achieved, chief/Big Man models of power and authority among the Tauade people, preferring a conception falling somewhere between an English-style landed gentleman and a rubbish-man, or *malavi*, presumably resting on a status distinction along with benevolent reciprocity. But patronage, while providing a means of implementing and reaffirming power and authority in eighteenth-century England, scarcely fits the power picture of Trobriander chiefs, which included tyranny, opposition, and conflict. While the English peasantry poached, stole lops, and wrote threatening letters to their betters, they did not practice sorcery against them, nor openly revolt to any appreciable extent. In time they were co-opted into an emerging ideology of law, which, oddly enough, entrapped the gentlemen who sought to impose it.

Public opinion became a force affecting the administration of law not only through gentlemanly legislation in the English parliament but also as a countervailing force available to the ordinary folk through the institution of the jury. There with the help and connivance of sympathetic judges and crown counsel, they mitigated and or completely disregarded the large numbers of capital offenses enacted by the landed gentry during the eighteenth century (Hall, 1935, pp. 133–152).

Validating Sorcery as Social Control

The general conclusion that sorcery was a conservative influence for many Melanesian societies is well documented. A number of writers, beginning with Malinowski's observations on the Trobrianders, have dwelled on this matter. Bowden (1987, p. 196) saw sorcery in a similar way, referring specifically to its use as arising out of "breaches of social norms," such as intrusion on secrets of the men's house, seduction of the daughter of a Mahoni, causing fires, abusing women, failing to pay debts, infringing on property rights, improper behavior at rituals, and inadequate contributions at ceremonial distributions (Chowning, N.D., pp. 158ff.). Other "breaches of social norms" provoking sorcery were alleged to be theft, incest, and failure to make bridal payments (Bowden, 1987, pp. 196ff.).

Fortune (1932, p. 175ff.) stated that the "Black art of the Dobuans was used not only to collect debts and enforce economic obligations but also to avenge one's own sickness or the death of kin." Dobuans also sorcerized to "wipe out any serious insult" and finally, "for the sake of trying it out." To these Todd (1935, p. 487) added "offenses" such as "defiance of a headman's authority . . ." more particularly "his undue display of wealth, and illicit sex relations with the wife of a man of rank by one of no substance."

A number of difficulties mar such forthright generalizations about sorcery as normative social control in Melanesia, among them the fact that not all societies there relied on sorcery for social control and some did not sanction its use. The Mae Enga, for example, blamed malevolent ghosts, deities, and demons, along with polluting women, for illness and death, beings whom they sought to avoid or propiate (Lawrence and Meggit, 1965, p. 129):

> Their view is that sorcery is an inefficient and somewhat immoral substitute for violence and economic sanctions in settling interpersonal and interclan disputes.

Ritual Validation of Sorcery as Social Control

Given the questionable influence of public opinion, if not the very existence of such a phenomenon in Melanesian communities, it still needs asking whether feelings of individuals towards sorcery might not have been aggregated by other organized means and sanctioned by other than "democratic" or political values. The closest approximation to validation of sorcery deaths as social control, comparable for example, to that found among the Zeltal (supra, 56) of Mexico, occurred among the Arapesh people of the Sepwich District of New Guinea (Tuzin, 1974, ch. 9) in the form of a Tambaran cult, dominated by old men through "consulting with ghosts." This conveyed the approval by a spirit figure *Nggwal*, of "one-half of all sorcery deaths in the community." The process called for the preparation of large amounts of food, mainly consumed by the gerontocracy that dominated the cult. What happened in cases of sorcery it left unapproved was not made clear, nor the attitudes of young men towards the gerontocrats.

Sorcery Inquests of the Gebusi

One other institutional practice related to general public opinion lay in sorcery inquests held by the Gebusi peoples and conducted as spirit seances led by specialized mediums. According to an enumeration by Knaupf (1985, p. 308), about one-fifth of such events dealt with responsibility for sorcery deaths.

Actually Gebusi held two kinds of inquiries. The first followed an all-night dance and ritual feast and took place in a "lower house," where men congregated to drink Kava. This occasion came closest to one notable for the free expression of opinion and for raising disputed matters, all mellowed by the mild euphoria of the drink. Problems of individuals, such as a sick son, an outsider who had fished out a man's stream, or a complaint that a spirit medium has not held a promised seance (p. 267) received free discussion. In some cases settlements were reached between disputants, at other times they were not. However, no anger followed, or better, no anger was generated. The feast maintained the appearance of "good fellowship" basic to the Gebusi ethos, expressed in male heterosexual and homosexual joking.[8]

---

8. Knaupf (p. 270) generalized that ritual feasts of the Gebusi served a Durkheimian function of creating social solidarity, particularly through sexual joking by the men. Based on my study of Kava drinking in Tonga, I am inclined to attribute the amity of the occasion to the effects of the Kava which is a mild soporific and hallucinogen. . . . In contrast to the effects of alcohol, Kava diminishes aggressive tendencies, so much so that it has been called the "peace drug of the Pacific." The report of sexual joking by the men is contrary to that of my informants who insisted, "Don't want women when you have Kava," a view verified by complaints of the wives of the drinkers. Most of the singular time lapse discussion I heard at Kava parties in Tonga and Suva dealt with very ordinary, even otherwise dull matters. See The Secular Use of Kava—with Special reference to Tonga (Lemert, 1967).

The sorcery inquest of the Gebusi, in contrast to that of the ritual feast, was lead by a spirit medium holding the equivalent of a seance in which joking, singing, and yelling took place. The songs shifted content from a spirit world to real-life events. According to the account, the inquests helped overcome anger but they also generated anger. Sorcery references and accusations emerged, but in a context of ambiguity, without consensus.

Following sorcery inquests, divinations were sought to identify the sorcerer. However, considerable time might pass until a group of men sought out and executed the supposed sorcerer. Sorcery deaths were not compensatable, so that suspects either had to be tolerated within the community, exiled, or executed. Living in another community did not solve the exile's poblems because his reputation followed him. If sago divinations proved unfavorable, the sorcerer likely met his death on the spot or was tortured through use of firebrands and then killed. In other cases, due to protection by his kinsmen, a lengthy delay preceded execution. Meantime the accuser worked to arouse anger in others to do the deed by staging a special seance for the purpose (p. 102).

Conclusions about Public Opinion
and Social Control

There is little doubt that in some Melanesians societies there were assemblies, particularly after Australian political control was established over their areas. There disputes got aired and discussion "led" under the direction of a councillor and a "committee." At least such was the case with moots on Matupit as reported by Epstein (1974, p. 109). Young, too (1974, pp. 142ff.), found that village meetings occurred among the Kalauna, which provided arenas for self-help and a forum for airing disputes and negotiating agreements. Generally speaking, however, authority began and ended with the convening of assemblies.

Only in rare cases did disputes get settled in a definitive way. Usually issues raised so involved other issues that agreements became impossible. Beyond this the issues tended to get politi-cized between clans and political cliques, leaving intransigent splits of opinion, at best creating divisions or detentes such as described by Young (1974, pp. 213ff.) following *abutus* among the Kalauna. Participants left meetings without indicating any resolutions of their conflicts; but over time some adaptations might transpire, without, however, any indications of how or why.

Epstein (1974, p. 108) stated that such assemblies could exert influence by means of public shame through references to moral norms and suggestions, but he gave no examples. At most, leaders encouraged settlements by mediation and negotiation much in the manner of Big Man intervention of an earlier era.

One suspects that Epstein may have idealized procedures of the moot with references to "mediation" since his characterizations of the appointed officials did not indicate any great commitment to their roles. Reay (1959, pp. 203ff.) wrote of the influence of certain men within clans and subclans. However, while they "steered opinion," they also "depended on opinion" for their eminence. Here as with Berndt's statements, we must take the author's assertion without specification of the referents for the term opinion, especially in regard to the land areas and issues within which it could operate without challenge.

6

Sorcery as a Legal Remedy

Berndt's interest in public opinion not only disposed him to see it as a validation of social control generally but also fathered his conclusion that it was the means by which sorcery became a legal remedy. The notion that sorcery or magic, at least in certain forms, was a conservative influence and a "tool of government" in primitive societies emerged as early as 1901 in a work by Hubert and Maus, *Theorie Generale de la Magic*, later reaffirmed by Frazer in *The Magic Art and the Evolution of Kings* (1922). Fortune (1932, p. 157) also recognized what struck him as a native awareness of law:

> It should be appreciated that there is a very strong legal background to the use of the black art. The natives understand how our legal system is imposed with the help of rifles perfectly. They say typically: "you have your rifles—we have tabu, witchcraft and sorcery, our weapons."

The full meaning of this excerpt is vague; Fortune merely assumed the existence of native law or a "legal system," something he did not put into evidence. Reduced to a minimum, Fortune said that natives he talked to saw a similarity in the use of collective force or coercion (phrased as weapons) to cause persons to avoid or comply with demands made by others. The implication that natives understood the nature of Australian law or its legal system is mainly testimony to Fortune's literary exuberance.

Evans-Pritchard on Sorcery
and Native Opinion

Chancing on Evans-Pritchard's 1931 article on "Sorcery and Native Opinion" briefly raised my hopes that his now older wisdom would help clarify the issue of the legal nature of magic and sorcery in relation to public opinion. Unfortunately his discussion comes through as a kind of survey of attitudes towards the use of sorcery rather than an analysis of their interplay. Thus he sorted out different kinds of sorcery and magic judged to be legal or not by native informants, with the purpose of testing Malinowski's contention that the "criminal" and the "legal" uses of sorcery could not be differentiated by reference to public opinion (p. 24). However, he omitted any comparative study on grounds that data were not available for the purpose, and drew only from his Azande findings.

From his limited interpretation Evans-Pritchard concluded that the natives, either by the use of "good/bad" terms or by their context, made it clear which was the case. Thus magic was not intrinsically bad or good because of its destructiveness but because it circumvented or flouted legal and moral rules of Azande society (p. 31):

> the vast majority of Zande magic ... receives the sanction of public approval and *approval of the chiefs* so long as it acts impartially according to the merits of the case between the magician and his object of vengeance.

The use of specific rituals for divination and judgments made in seances plus beliefs that ill-used magic turned against its user gave magic its validity or its "justice." The term for illegal magic was *sorcery*. In particular the use of *menzele* medicine (murder magic) was absolutely abhorred by all, and any Azande using it was invariably executed unless he was of noble blood. Even the most powerful chiefs feared such sorcery. The illegality of other medicines such as *mota orgho* depended on the opinion of the chiefs.

In sum, magic took on institutionalized form through fixed individual and collective rituals that were approved by chiefs and princes, elites, and heads of a conquest state.[1]

What can be said comfortably is that the Azande as well as other African peoples living in such states recognized ascriptive authority. While the use of magic emerged from self-help, it was implicitly as well as explicitly authorized, much in the manner of early Roman law in which the *praetor* simply gave the sanction of law by ratifying actions already carried out self-help style. Authority rather than public opinion legitimated such actions as law.

Sorcery, Secrecy, and Legality

Although ethnographers may write of its legality it is unlikely that Melanesians themselves had a concept of legitimate sorcery, certainly not the Kalauna, according to Young (1974, p. 127). The most telling criticism of the assumed legality of sorcery is its secrecy—this in contrast to Western law which is a public process, open to inspection and recorded, features inherent in its requirement for authoritative promulgation. In contrast, the secrecy of sorcery is an essential element in its efficacy. Sorcerers seldom talked about their machinations. Gossip, when it occurred, started with sickness or deaths, but agreement as to their causes might or might not follow. Mistaken guesses could lead to vain efforts at compensation. Accusation of sorcery did not routinely create consensus in individual cases although this might happen in situations involving a number of deaths, likely to arouse widespread fears or activate a feud.

Sorcery opinion, as with opinion on other matters, tended to be confined to concerned groups, who, as noted previously, might or might not be moved to some action. There are indications that strictures limited their talk about sorcery. Indeed one may go so far as to propose that a kind of etiquette of sorcery talk generally constrained and structured expressions on the subject. Fortune (1932, pp. 45ff.) tells how his personal boys were

---

1. For an account of a formal trial procedure dealing with suspected witches in the former African state of Tonja, see Goody, Esther; supra, 57.

"viciously corrective" of him for making simple inquiries about persons involved in witchcraft:

That is a thing that is never done—to *hawawerebana*, talk specifically of witchcraft and infer the witch. Haven't you got any sense! The Dobuans considered it a most serious insult to refer to a woman's witchcraft so that her husband will hear of it.

Apart from talk tabus about sorcery Melanesians had no secular procedures for establishing a factual basis for action against an accused person. This was one of the main criticisms that Seagle (1937) brought against Malinowski's claim for the existence of law among the Trobrianders, in particular the notion that sorcery was a legal influence. His objection emphasized that sorcery involved supernatural, unseen forces whose manipulation is a nonsecular process (p. 232):

For this reason, sorcery although it may be a very potent force in primitive society, is not properly to be regarded as a legal influence even when it is used as a method of retaliation for injuries in this world.

Llewellyn and Hoebel (1941, p. 314) were essentially in agreement with Seagle as to the legal influence of sorcery, at least as it operated among the Cheyenne:

we recall that sorcery of high power was known to them, but we find no trace of its use in legal matters, unless the white magic of detection by way of dreams to guide the finding of evidence, be such a trace. Otherwise the makeshift "resource of the weak" which can so easily become scourge to all or any, was absent; as in a sound juristic system it should be.

A final inconsistent note in the arguments for the legality of sorcery lay in the irregular, one-sided motives of envy and jealousy and unprovoked meanness that prompted its use. Still another note, higher in the scale, came from the use of sorcery by Big Men, who, at certain stages of their careers employed it as a political tool for a variety of purposes.

Social Control and Law: An Excursus

To pursue the argument that sorcery is a legal remedy made so by public opinion in some ways is to trivialize the question of the existence of primitive law generally and particularly so in Melanesia. In a larger mode of inquiry into the matter of primitive law one may ask, rhetorically at least, whether pristine Melanesian societies more than any others did not resonate the Hobbesian query as to how social order is achieved, given the highly competitive nature of their peoples, their cultural emphasis on equivalence, their relative lack of and distaste for formal leadership, and their zest for warfare.

While the "war of all against all" may overstate the case for precontact New Guinea societies, nevertheless wanton "killing for the sake of killing," not excluding women and children, stood high among their values (Barnes, 1962). An informal account by a Big man, himself a warrior, portrays a New Guinea version of the "killing fields" (Onaka, 1979, pp. 49ff.):

> We watched our chance and when they were involved in a fight elsewhere, we went to help their enemies, we cut their bananas [trees], raped their women and burnt their houses . . . twenty men might lay hold of the same woman, pulling her round for a day and a night. . . .

While social disorders born of war and feuding in Melanesia were largely external in nature, it was equally true that communities suffered from problems of "internal regulation" (Young, 1974, p. 114). Intragroup conflict was endemic as well, not only between political units but even reaching down to more intimate group levels. Hobbes' version of the rational man come to succor the Melanesians from their "brutal, nasty, short lives" was not to be fulfilled. Rather such order as came to be in New Guinea and Papua derived from the Australian government, entrusted with control over the area in 1948 by the United Nations.

While Australian colonial administrators ultimately if sporadically suppressed warfare in the mandated areas and natives acquired access to courts Australian style, questions about the feasibility and nature of social control by law persisted. Some writers laid the uncertainty to the neglect by anthropologists, who produced only a meager literature on the subject, with additional blame left over for the territorial government. But as Epstein (1974) makes clear, the more important problem may have been the "crazy-quilt," amorphous, acephalous, and demographically mixed and mixing nature of Melanesian societies.

Presumably such considerations lay behind the shift of interests of anthropologists in Melanesia from customary law formulations to studies of conflict resolution, reflected in publication of the book *Contention and Dispute in 1974*, a product of a 1969 conference on the subject of native law.

In their favor it must be said that anthropologists at work in Melanesia gave more detailed attention and substance to the concept of social control than did their confreres working in Africa; but their endeavors, especially in reports making up *Contention and Dispute in 1974*, continued to be marred by subsuming or construing social control as law. To be sure, this could have stemmed from ambiguity in the concept of social control, but it also owed a great deal to an overriding concern of a number of anthropologists, most conspicuously beginning with Malinowski, to show if not prove that preliterate people have law generically similar to that of Western societies. In any case the 1969 conference alluded to here, despite the apparent assignment to focus on dispute settlement, had numerous references to law in the societies discussed, even to the extent of asserting that Melanesians do have law, but that it is just different from that of the West. Beyond this some participants went so far as to insist that Melanesians have legal concepts similar to those of Anglo-Saxon derived laws. This came out in a report on the Kalai Lupunga (Epstein, 1974, ch. 4) in which the authors blandly asserted that disputes arose over the violation of personal and property rights. Granting that the Kalai do not use such terms, the authors nevertheless proceeded to tabulate such rights of individuals—essentially those recognized historically in English law and enumerated in the American Bill of Rights (pp. 128ff.).

Such an exercise sheds very little light on the Melanesian dispute process, since it is doubtful whether counselors, mediators, or contenting parties either understood or had any interest in rights so conceived. Their motives had to do with restoring order and besting the other party, if not actually making trouble for the other party in a devious way.

The Quest for Law

Considerable virtuosity has marked the efforts of anthropologists to find equivalents of Western law in primitive societies—in equating Eskimo drum contests with courts or legal proceedings, making symbolic drawing of a bow commensurate with legal coercion, and finally, referring to sorcery as a legal remedy. Gluckman (1975) went farthest in pressing legal analogies across cultures, urging that the Barotse judges in Lotse land (Africa) invoked many salient ideas or procedures common to Western jurisprudence, particularly that of the "reasonable man."

My askance here does not imply that there are no precursors of modern Western law to be found in low-energy, nonliterate societies. Rather it is to recall that the comparative method deals with differences as well as similarities. In the case of the Barotse this demands attention to a context in which judges sat with a king, simultaneously served as councillors, legislators, and administrators, as well as being spokesmen for religion.[2]

Questing for law Western style in simpler societies mounts problems of effacing the critical mode in favor of trying to prove something. In so doing it may exclude regulatory phenomena ethnographers may want to study, or that collators of their studies may want to know about. It was for these reasons that Llewellyn (1940, p. 1286) chose not to define law, and simply referred to "legal matters"—a stance that allowed him to range widely in his research, use his own form of discourse, and to

---

2. The critical literature on Gluckman's ideas is well known. I merely observe that for Barotse judges "reasonable" meant "moral" or "conformist"; i.e., they did not separate law and morality. That Western law differs sharply in this respect is suggested not only by Holmes (1897) timeless essay on the subject but also by Gluckman's own observations on the subject, namely that the Lotse ". . . found the work of the British courts . . . alien and incomprehensible to them."

see the administration of the law as a juristic art as well as a form of social control.

Llewellyn properly emphasized the difficulty of adapting social science to research on law, due to its contorted context, "making Western law a world of its own—a sort of unchartable fourth dimensional space, alien to laymen, but also to specialist, in the social disciplines" (Llewellyn and Hoebel, 1941, p. 41).

Llewellyn (1940), in contrast to those anthropologists who tried to cast relatively simple ideas about social control into law, sought to reduce its study to a kind of Celtic simplicity with such neologisms as "law jobs," "law stuff," "trouble cases," and "operative facts."

Girded with these terms, Llewellyn took up the task set by Roscoe Pound, that of distinguishing the symbol from the *acta*—law in action from law on the books. This drew attention away from doctrine *per se* to socio-legal processes, set in motion where there is deviance, dispute, or "hitch" in human social interaction. From this view it is not enough to define law as rules, precepts, ideas, or principles apart from their institutional substance or from their processual context. Nor should one seperate social control from law, which Llewellyn (1940) construed as the normative and the legal, whose boundaries overlap and shift, depending on cultural change, from which may erupt trouble cases.

Young (1974, p. 115) came closest to a dynamic analysis of social control similar to that advocated by Llewellyn. From his Kalauna data he more or less independently validated Roscoe Pound's insistence that legal analysis dealt with interests rather than principles:

> Delicts rather than crimes and sins are what concern Kalauna people. An important corollary of this is that interests rather than principles are at stake in the majority of disputes. Another is that it is not what one does but whom he does it to that matters, for not all persons have equal access to the same sanctions . . . it is of little value to generalize that 'theft' is punished by public shaming, adultery is punished by court action, often following

abutus, or that "failure to follow food-sharing obligations" is punished by sorcery.[3]

The uncritical application of Western penal code and other
legal terms to native delicts leaves awkward questions as to what
is being controlled, who does the controlling, by what means,
and with what effects. Missing elements in the usages of Melanesian ethnographers concern whether the behavior is constrained,
redirected, or changed. Nor is it always clear whether outcomes
deemed to be social control are punishment, redress, control,
or merely the futile expression of anger and discord.

Illustrative ambiguities on these scores come from an early
report attributing the use of legal fines to tribes on the D'Entrecasteaux archipelago. Close reading of the report indicates that
fines turn out to be redress in kind, such as yams, bananas, tools,
or weapons, negotiated through the "manipulative, bargaining
approach common to the natives of New Guinea" (Stanner, 1959,
p. 216; Young, 1974, p. 115). The sanction behind the negotiation
was the threat of violence, supported by the victim's kin, who
stood to share in the spoils. But for this very reason intraclan
delicts might go unpunished because the aggressor stood to
benefit as well as his kin. Application of such redress to wrongs
such as rape, assault, and even murder makes its resemblance
to modern fines even more remote.[4]

Harangues, to choose one among such sanctions, got
delivered at night in front of the angry man's dwelling, or at a
public meeting. The object of the victim's wrath, in many but
not all instances, simply withdrew from his place of residence
for a period of time or permanently. Exile, if that's what it was,
was self-imposed. For Melanesians it lacked the force of tribal
expulsion found among the Barama River Caribs, which usually
meant death by starvation in the unforgiving bush (supra, 42).

Insistence on revising or reinterpreting terms such as *fines*
and *exile* according to the specifics of context and action becomes

---

3. Epstein (1984) makes a similar point by insisting that the details and context
must be given for complete analysis of social control.

4. Counts (1974, p. 118) wrote of exile by the Kalai Lupunga people as an extreme
measure for recusants, who "drained the resources" and threatened the unity and safety
of the *kambu.* However, it was rarely used.

more than a quibble over words if Epstein's (1984) thesis is correct, that shame underlies much of social control in Melanesia.

One might even argue that its importance in some forms has grown with the acquisition of metal tools and implements since contact with the Australian government and foreign traders, notable for example, in the aggrandizing of the *abutu* and fesivals of the Kalauna (Young, 1974).

In keeping with this efflorescence of organized shaming, or even because of it, Australian law and legal organization has had relatively little effect on Melanesian methods of social control. The gulf separating Australian law and Melanesian methods of social control, and the attendant difficulties of trying to impose one on the other, was quite early recognized by Seagle (1946) in his pithy commentary originally directed at Malinowski's findings about law among the Trobrianders:

> an older caution still seems pertinent; it is indeed important in writing of primitive law not to stretch it upon the procrustean bed of modern legal concepts.

An equally strong statement appeared in the introduction to the report of a 1969 conference on the law problems of New Guinea held at the Australian National University, a statement that noted (Sawyer, p. 10):

> the social tension inherent in an attempt to apply Western legal concepts and institutions in a tribal society which has fewer features of what the West calls law than have the indigenes of almost any other areas aspiring to independent existence as an organized state in the world.

An equally lucid statement on the same subject can be found in the same introduction (Sawyer, p. 16):

> Ausralian type legal system, and Australia and New Guinea represent quite different, specialized social systems, each with its own highly idiosyncratic process of social control geared to operate within it and meet its peculiar needs.

While some incidentally valid uses may be made by Melanesians of Australian imposed court procedures, on the whole, the natives, like those faced with Anglo-Saxon type law in other parts of the world, such as India (Cohn, 1975, pp. 139ff.), either try to exploit the system or stand aloof from it. Threats to take disputes to Australian courts, while effective in part, suffer from diminishing returns if not carried out.

The crucial missing features in social control exercised by Melanesians that might otherwise qualify it as law are:

1. The absence of established or institutionalized authority with power to make and enforce decisions within given jurisdictions; i.e., no legislators, judges or magistrates.
2. The lack of courts with fixed procedures to determine evidence.
3. The lack of any written laws or those perpetuated by oral lawgiver.
4. The absence of a concept of crime, i.e., felony.

The gross difference between Western law and social control in New Guinea societies can be phrased even more succinctly in terms of its aims (Brown, 1966, pp. 33–34):

Western law seeks to restore or guarantee individual and equal rights. The stress is on abstract justice, and impartial punishment according to the nature of the actions of the parties.

Cultural Relativity and the Realities of Evil

Although I have tried to stay close to the idea of evil as an experience commanding empirical study, my progress, if that it be, through the ethnographic literature on Melanesian societies has led me to think in a less cavalier manner about the possible substantive nature of evil. My ensuing queries, however, need not revert to philosophical or religious discourse, nor need conclusions become unrestrained subjectivism. They start with a brief consideration of the idea of cultural relativity.

Sociology, anthropology, and psychology all have been influenced by what in the early twentieth century came to be a readily accepted, easily mouthed credo, "cultural relativity." American anthropologists—Kroeber, Lowie, and others of the so-called critical historical school through linguistic and other space-time specified studies—had by 1930 pretty well demolished the early cultural evolutionary theories of Morgan and others. Somewhat earlier, in 1920, reactions to political and economic disturbances in the United States had given sinister overtones to the idea of evolution, and progress, colored, if I may use the term, by "red scares" of the period (Cottrell, 1972).

Beginning in the 1930s a small but captious efflorescence of textbooks in sociology and anthropology documented the idea that cultures of primitive peoples had an integrity of their own, understandable in the context of their own environments. Adaptation replaced scientifically directed progress as a key term in the transformation of social thought, and the word "primitive" was replaced by the more politically correct but awkward "preliterate" to designate its subject matter.

All of this had its organizational parallel with the appearance of joint departments of anthropology and sociology that granted combined degrees, most conspicuous at the Department of Social Relations at Harvard University. Translation of Max Weber's works into English at this time and embracing his notion of "value free analysis" helped to validate sociology's aspirations to status as a science. A final stamp of orthodoxy came with the movement to convert sociology into science more or less framed with mid-nineteenth-century conceptions of fixed relationships between cause and effect, ceding no compromise with the idea that human choices influence the course of cultural development.

In anthropology, ethical relativism, sometimes separated from cultural relativism, owed much of its early currency to the writings of Mead and Benedict. Mead (1961) achieved auctorial fame by popularizing a permissive view of adolescent sex indulgence, "love under the palm trees," in Samoa as a wholesome alternative to the *sturm und drang* of American teenage transition to adulthood. That her findings, which pertained to a small island of Manua, removed in space and time from the main populations of Uppolu and Savaii in Samoa, might be questionable, did not surface until years later.

Benedict (1934), who wrote eloquently of diametrically opposed culture patterns of Native Americans, merely noted "the coexisting and equivalent verbal patterns of life which mankind had carved for itself from the raw materials of existence." A sociologist, Hartung (1954), even more blandly asserted that if people approved of a practice it was as good as any other. Hoebel (1968, p. 473) stressed the need for tolerance in a conflict-torn world. These and other equally simple rationales served to perpetuate an uncritical view of the transcultural worth of various social practices initiated by the demise of evolutionary thought.

World War II and after gave pause to the cultural relativists, mainly from media exposure of Nazi atrocities, along with those brought to light in the disastrous war of the United States with Viet Nam and the outcome of Russia's unhappy military adventure into Afghanistan. The growth of nationalism and the dismal record of foreign aid programs demanded a "change of interpretation," rather than more facts about cross-cultural evaluations.

Meantime the in-stock ideas of Krober, Redfield, White, Sapir, and others provided a fall back, modified evolutionary perspective on the ethical issues of transcultural differences. Going beyond a changed perspective to a workable formulation of the problem proved no simple matter. After his survey of the literature Kluckhohn (1955, p. 152) offered "two fairly cheerful propositions" on the matter: (1) that cross-cultural communication is possible once core likenesses are disentangled, and (2) that acceptance of science as a method requires that more postulates be in accord with its findings.

The more onerous task of elaborating the specifics of such cross-cultural communication fell to Linton (1954, pp. 150–152) who drew on his considerable knowledge of world cultures to reach a conclusion, with which, according to Kluckhohn, anthropologists "could feel comfortable," namely that cross-cultural likenesses are primarily conceptual and that "variation rages rampant as to details of prescribed practices, instrumentalities and sanctions."

However, as I try to show in an article on "Issues in the Study of Deviance" (Lemert, 1981), if norms are inferred from reactions of social control rather than conceptual statements, the problem is clouded and complicated by variations in social definitions and sanctions actually invoked in particular social situations. This stands out very clearly in failed past attempts to discover a universal conception of crime, a point on which criminologists are agreed (Znaniecki, 1960). Much the same can be said generally for "deviance from norms." Most frequently it has been the specifics of social control that become a litmus test of conclusions about the ethics of primitive peoples.

Making Transcultural Judgments

Social scientists can make comparative judgments about native cultures with several purposes in mind: (1) to aid or assist the native peoples in question to "develop" economically and to adapt to problems created by contact with Western peoples, (2) to ascertain in scientific terms whether their practices are maladaptive or, (3) self-defeating when projected against the values, goals, and ends of the native cultures themselves.

Generally speaking, the record of foreign aid programs has fallen short of Kluckhohn's (1952) optimism about cross-cultural communication, largely due to vested economic interests of their sponsors and lack of feedback from target populations (Hirts, F., 1992). In any case, interest here rests with items two and three, especially the last. Melanesians scored abysmally low on their quality of life (Weidman, H. and Sussex, J. M., 1971).

More direct and pertinent comparisons of cultures remain a difficult challenge for psychological anthropologists, who must somehow deal with criticisms of older culture/personality theories that advanced a classification on a shame/guilt emphasis. One recent approach, that of Edgerton (1992) boldly applies psychiatric diagnoses to cultures; but despite his extensive documentation, readers may be left to wonder whether he overcomes the criticism of reductionism that haunts such theory. One difficulty lies in the confusion between normal, that is, socially acceptable, delusional beliefs and those of mentally ill persons.

A similar kind of analysis by Schwartz (1973, p. 156) recognized the danger of applying individual psychology to a society or to a culture, but nevertheless used a conception of paranoia to depict the ethos of Melanesian societies. The core of this conception lay in the interplay of fear, distrust, and "sensitivity to intentions and submerged meanings of others," along with the justified "defense of each man" (p. 157) against the perceived reality of sorcery attacks and the "real danger of physical attacks."

However insightful this summary statement may be, it does not account for discrepancies of behavior related to the interaction of individuals and political groups, much of which in Melanesia, as in early Hawaii, is conveyed in metaphoric language, which was greatly influenced by historical allusions dating back to incidents as old as thirty years or more. To cite Lederman (1986, p. 189) on this matter:

> Events that occur during wealth displays in Mendi are frequently interpreted to mean something other than what they are manifestly about. . . .Sometimes people are credited with saying or doing one thing publicly in order to convey another message indirectly, in a subtle manner that may bring important matters to people's attention for informal discussion later on, while avoiding direct public confrontation. Natural occurrences may become objects of metaphoric reference and interpretation.

A net result of Mendi ambiguity in communication was the acceptance of a tribal or clan purpose coupled with contrary actions related to obligations of individuals to their exchange partners. All of this is quite different from exclusion of diagnosed paranoid persons from intimate social interaction, which I described in my article on "Paranoia and the Dynamics of Exclusion" (Lemert, 1972).

Value Conflicts and Cyclical Expression of Evil

One alternative to straining the interpretive possibilities of psychiatric diagnostic categories for studying collective actions of Melanesians is to pursue the consequences of paramount or patterned values conflicts, particularly as they impinge on the roles of warriors and Big Men. Evil rather than pathology informs such analysis, best shown by a diachronic rather than synchronic perspective.

To a greater or lesser degree a number of Melanesian societies appear to have been caught up in cycles of low-level warfare, interpersonal violence, cannibalism, and homicide. Atomism of feeling, thought, and action often prevailed, typified in sharp relief among the Tauade people, who enacted patterns of outrage, violence, and retaliation, followed by compensation. Because interaction was defined in material terms by what Hallpike (1977, ch. III) called Heroclitean mentality, it produced no more than ephemeral equilibrium, but not harmony, which led him to class Tauade society as a "model of disintegration—the theme of this book" (p. 98).

Feasts, dances, and the disposition of pigs by the Tauade combined to reinforce a regressive interaction so that trade or gift exchanges became sources of conflict, leading to crises and vengeance that made corporate life hazardous and contracted its elements to small security circles. The resultant social cycles of killings, vengeance, then escalation of violence of incidental killings, by chance or choice had its reciprocal in the ebb and flow of emotions in individuals. Asked for the reason for their killings, one Tauade warrior replied (p. 208):

> You know our fashion. We look at these people. We look at these people we look at them for a long time. We say they are there; good, we will kill them. We think of this all the time and when our bellies get too hot we go to kill them.

Passions of individuals in Tauade society were not socially defined as destructive, deviant, or pathological, but rather were looked on as the generative stuff of social interaction. Anger, deliberate and malicious interference with a dance, or demanding gift compensation for imagined slights did not provoke overt disapproval or sanctions.

The atomism of Tauade life and knowledge that delicts could be compensated left individuals relatively free of social control.

Apart from shaming, which occurred after the fact, there existed no way for a tribe or clan effectively to control aggression of individual members; at the same time vengeance for their acts could fall on any member of their own tribe, which extended the scope of conflict. One measure of the fatal consequence of the absence of effective social control showed in the fact that one-half of those killed were intratribal members.

A veneer of reserve, repressed anger and fierce pride as a defense against a hostile world marked the demeanor of the Tauade warrior. Downgrading others to gain an emotional advantage, contempt for weakness, sensitivity to insult, and enjoyment of the discomfiture of their competitors stood out as conspicuous features of Tauade social interaction. The economics of exchange was subordinated in their value hierarchies to other considerations:

These were no sober agriculturalists, making narrow calculations of profit and loss to better their circumstances, but savage men in the grip of a collective obsession with blood and death. (p. 252)

Warfare and Evil

While some ambiguity lurks in the literature on Melanesian warfare (Knauft, 1990), there can be little doubt that it was a source of motivation to excel and of consummate pleasure. Moreover, in some societies, it was a means of transcendence expressed in cultlike beliefs and myths, such as that of the war god of peoples on Normandy Island (Röheim, 1946). Ruthless killing, torture of captives, cannibalism, even the sale of human flesh made up a pattern probably unmatched for its cultivated cruelty. Warriors of Dobu in some instances grew so fond of eating human flesh as to describe their tastes in true gourmet style (p. 231):

their way of killing and eating human flesh showed an utter lack of compunction in this matter . . . it was cannibalism accompanied by cultivated and finished cruelties without which the full enjoyment of the horrible

feast was not attained. Not infrequently a living victim
would be hung over a fire, his cries being greeted with
delight by surrounders, who proceeded to beat him to
death while catching the warm blood from wounds and
drinking it on the spot.

This author interpreted texts about the war god *Yaboaine* as
symbolic of a deep-seated anxiety within Dobuan men, particularly when they "shouted up" to their God after capturing
an enemy, which they equated with capturing a pig or growing
prize yams. These warriors shouted to refute any aspersion
against their fame by insisting that, "if we are only weak warriors
you should take us up in the sky and send better ones down."
In so doing they combined diffidence with anxiety in a self-
defensive ritual, elaborated when one warrior donned a skirt,
playfully recognizing that failure to have captured their victim
would cause others to call them women. Thus by denying that
they are men, they dealt with the anxiety created by their
aggression.

This analysis essentially reduces the Dobuan war culture
of vicious aggression and desecration of enemies to psychological, and in this case, psychoanalytic ideas. It bypasses or
ignores results of the absence of social controls to repress
violence, the cultural reliance on the malicious motivation of
sorcery to compel compensation, and the possible effectiveness
of shaming which turns anger in on the self.

Yet this manner of thought tells a good deal about "negative"
emotions and their playful dramatization as an intrinsic part
of the self, which in various forms characterizes the social
psychology of peoples of Southeast Asia. Recently social scientists have begun to realize the insufficiency of G. H. Mead's
philosophy of the act as part of the "inner forum of thought"
based on the study of symbols defined as behavioral gestures.
This view, which admitted the existence of a dynamic, biological
"I," in contrast to the "me," nevertheless took it for granted or
simply assumed it as a constant. Its limitations for sociopsychological research across cultures has only begun to be appreciated.

Kumagi (1988) has offered the most readily understood study
of the focal importance of the psychobiological or the assessed

energy component in Japanese self-conceptions. Her study, based on observation of childhood socialization and language usages, sums up its place in the Japanese self as *Ki*, of which the individual is continuously aware, and is uppermost in his/her motivation to meet group-defined task expectations and fulfil mutual obligations to others.

While Kumagi's analysis readily extends in a generic sense to peoples of Southeast Asia, its application and outcome differ, especially in relation to the place of violence in social relations. Thus, homicide rates, based on admittedly crude data, are spectacularly higher in some Melanesian societies, such as the Gebusi, than those in Japan, or even in the United States and Latin American countries (Knauft, 1985, p. 379).

I submit that in contrast to the cultures of the Melanesians, that of Japan, while it stresses achievement, reserves its highest acclaim for transcendent loyalty and purity of motivation, things strongly emphasized in child socialization as well as featured in Japanese legends and literature. Thus, excess finds full acceptance in Japan as well as in Melanesia, but it may be shown by failure as well as success (Morris, 1975).

It is also true that Japanese compartmentalize their sex behavior and normalize drunkenness. This diminishes conflict over adultery and other moral concerns, such as nudity, pornography, and prostitution. Hot baths, massages, and gambling help reduce the high tension levels of their daily lives. In these regards the contrast with Melanesian cultures is striking, for Melanesians appear to have few diversionary activities apart from kava drinking in some areas. Their rituals, feasts, and dances often created rather than reduced stress and tension.

It is difficult to say for certain whether the purity of motivation idealized by the Japanese has a counterpart in Melanesian values. The question gets obscured and complicated by the presence of sorcery, whose hidden nature for Melanesians symbolized the malicious side of openly expressed feelings and emotions, best exemplified by the "good company" ethos of the Gebusi people. To some extent the ideal of purity of motives may inhere in the values of equivalence common to many Melanesian societies, which finds clearest expression in the interaction of exchange partners. In a less obvious way it may be seen in the conflicting actions of Big Men.

Big Men and Evil

If evil suffused the Melanesian warrior role it also insinuated the careers of Big Men, who served as managers of gift exchanges; organized house building, feasts, dances, and other ceremonies; and also mediated disputes. Although there is some debate on the point, men became Big Men largely through managerial skills.

In some ways the Melanesian manager resembled a Western politician, as a kind of "wheeler and dealer" who employed oratory, promises and favors, and "cut corners" to outdo his rivals. To cite Burridge (1965–66, p. 93):

> On one hand he had to restrain self willedness and conform to moralities; on the other hand if he was to remain in control of a developing com-sensus he had to cheat a little, go outside the normative realities.

Speaking of Mt. Hagen societies, Strathern (1966, p. 365) tells us:

> It is well known that some Big Men are expert "greasers," that they try to cheat partners by promising fine returns and then defaulting or substituting poor goods, or that they may try to bully little men into giving up gifts and then attempt to ignore the debt entirely.

Big Men, Power and Evil

The career history of Big Men of Melanesia, as with some Paiute shaman and Tlingit chiefs referred to previously, adds truth to the idea that with passing time, power, whether resting on charisma, reification, or mystical beliefs, tends to corrupt those who use it. While followers could call Big Men to account, apparently this was not easy to do. To quote Burridge on this (1975, pp. 96–99):

The Manager had networks of friends, kin and trading partners in different villages. He could provoke incidents leading to homicide and control the consequences of accusations of sorcery and of real or alleged homicide . . . he also created sanctuaries from homicide and sorcery . . . the situation created feelings of smooth roguery, all the more dastardly and informed with spite when it seemed that smooth roguery was being answered with sorcery causing sickness that would lead to accusation of sorcery, injuries and homicide.

Resort to sorcery usually came at high points of the Big Man's career, when "he met the limits of his prestige" from exchange relationships. At this time others more readily suspected that this was the case, which brought the manager a new problem of resolving the contradictions of being a conscientious leader with that of a sorcerer. Thus Big Men of Melanesia, in a figurative sense, operated astride two diametrically opposed major strains of values in their cultures: competitive achievement and equivalence. Being so positioned generated acute self-awareness, intensified by the use of sorcery as well as trading in its materials. In this vein Read (1959, p. 434) relates how Big Men described themselves as "bad men," concluding that their behavior showed small concern for virtues they attempted to instill in others. Yet this reflexive sensitivity to inconsistencies of their culture gave them the insight that selected them as leaders.[5]

My reading of the accounts of three others among the societies cited by Knauft, combined with Hoebel's critique of Malinowski's early claims on the issue, leaves me unconvinced that sorcery was or is amenable to monopoly, legitimation, or effective social control. In the one replication study (rare in ethnography) of the Mekeo by Stephen (1987, ch. 2) there is no indication that sorcerers served as "policemen" for chiefs,

---

5. Knauft (1985, p. 343) objected to Burridge's word portrait of the Big Man on grounds that it ignored the variations in a number of Melanesian societies, starting with the Trobrianders among whom, so said Knauft, sorcery was effectively controlled by "stable leadership."

as asserted by Hau'ofa (1971). While Stephen's closely studied sorcerer was chief of his own descent group, he associated with only a very few people, certainly not with those in other men's houses, and there is no mention of contact with other chiefs. Without further laborious citations I simply note my reasons for questioning Knauft's "ethnographic conclusions" about the control of sorcery: (1) reliance an Hau'ofa's "idealized picture," of the Mekeo in which "detailed operation of the system was not dealt with" (p. 152); (2) the secrecy surrounding the use of sorcery; (3) willingness of sorcerers to teach their techniques to others, probably as a way of diffusing suspicion or directing it away from themselves; (4) sorcery was taught by fathers to sons; (5) the scope of authority of hereditary chiefs was limited as to areas and acivities; (6) a hereditary chief could and did lose his influence and followers much like the Big Man. Zelenietz (1981, p. 4) presented the issue well when he referred to the "perennial problem in the study of sorcery: the diversity of data available and the multiplicity of conclusions we may draw from these data . . . [which] gives the social anthropologist the capability to support almost any generalization or set of contradictory general-izations." In this light it seems to me that in citing Erikson's (1966) theory of deviance and labeling, Knauft subscribed to functionalist theory that has lost its place in sociological thought.

The Sorcerer's Role as Evil

The Melanesian sorcerer, more than anyone else, personified unmitigated evil even though at times he practiced counter-sorcery. Certainly he was not seen as a healer comparable to medicine men and shamans. If Stephen's (1987, ch. 2) portrayal is valid, the sorcerer was concerned to achieve transcendent contact with the spirit world by self-isolation and self-medication. His black clothing and cadaverous appearance associated him in the minds of others with the night, the threatening, and the dangerous. Burridge (1965–66) spoke of the moral consequences of his behavior and status (p. 96):

He who behaved as a sorcerer might . . . be treated as a sorcerer. Murderer, trespasser and scapegoat, 'sorcerer' was often a label looking for a man. He who labelled himself was feared and differentially treated.

People most actively feared sorcerers from other villages, based on the assumption that local sorcerers concentrated their evil influences on outsiders—again, an attitude sorcerers were unlikely to discourage since it helped to protect them from suspicion and secure their status.

To a degree difficult to specify, Melanesian sorcerers resembled those who do "dirty work" necessary in Western societies; their actions were cloaked by their low social visibility and social isolation due to fear and ambivalent attitudes of others who typically avoided them.

The power of sorcerers thus was enhanced by conditions that left them relatively unaccountable for their acitons. In this respect Melanesian sorcerers differed from the shamans among the Yokuts-Mono, among whom the natives could distinguish honest doctors from those who exploited their secret powers.

Attitudes Towards Sorcery

There are only scattered references to the attitudes of Melanesians towards sorcery, mostly reflecting the notion that because of its value for social control it was a necessary evil. Looked at more closely, the justification or belief does not stand up very well. For one thing, as already noted, some Melanesian peoples such as the Mae Enga did not rely on sorcery for social control; they regarded its use as immoral and managed to get along without it.

In societies where sorcery did prevail, attitudes are probably best described as ranging from ambivalent to disapproval. This negative tilting of opinion impressed Young (1971, p. 133), who summarized the disapproval and sense of threat from sorcery felt by Kalauna natives as follows:

few would go so far as to pretend it (sorcery) was a "beneficent agency." It needs hardly to be said that more suffering is attributed to sorcery than to any other cause.

Moreover, the psychological strain of living in such a sorcery-ridden community is considerable, especially since there are so few degrees of kinship within which the occurence of sorcery is unthinkable.

This characterization fits well with Marwick's (1964, p. 263) likening of the preoccupation with sorcery to a "social strain gauge." The comparison has a special aptness when it is incorporated with the idea of fluctuating intensity in the course of sorcery fears, ranging from low-level to heights of panic. Some notions of the latter comes from a survey reported by Tompkinson (1981, pp. 83ff.) of popular reactions in Southern Ambryn, Vanatu:

of 45 men interviewed, 36 reported at least one sorcery attack with themselves as possible victims. 3/4 attributed it to disturbances due to: disputes over women, over land boundaries or coconuts, and possible offense given to chiefs. 2/3 of those concerned were alerted by *Lele* [diviners], or by kin, or friends who "heard rumors"; 3 [persons] recognized omens, as, for example, the sudden death of a prized pig.

At this period "when sorcery was rife" some men reacted by locking themselves in their houses and restricted movements by their families. Others, if they believed that they had offended someone, paid compensation; and still others paid money or gave liquor to chiefs.

The Limited Efficacy
of Sorcery as Social Control

I find it difficult to accept the above reporter's interpretation of these behaviors as evidence of the "eufunctional aspects" of sorcery that discourages deviant behavior and encourages balance in reciprocity. This is because no showing is made either of the behavior controlled nor of the specifics of the reciprocity. An alternative interpretation is that a period "rife" with sorcery is likely to generate a great deal of irrational behavior (meaning disproportionate reactions to situations) random in nature on the part of those who deem themselves at risk.

A more precise criticism of the extent to which sorcery "functions" as social control comes from Young (1971, p. 129) who stated that for it to control others, the "victim" would have to know that the magical actions had been performed, that they were directed at him, and that they required redress. Examining Young's sample of cases revealed that these conditions were met in less than one-quarter of reported sorcery attacks. Even allowing for the possibility of secret quarrels, it is plain that social control by sorcery was more a matter of fear born of plural ignorance and random gossip than of knowable acts by others.

If this is right, then the ambience of sorcery did more to reinforce fear by rumor than it did to produce substantial redress. Indeed, fear actually diminished reciprocity when persons were afraid to complain about the value of gifts they received lest they become a sorcerer's victim. I can also conceive that some obligated persons found the situation favorable for exploitation, not only cheating on obligations but profiting from misdirected fears.

As far as one can tell, these problems did not vitiate the passive control pattern of the Yokuts-Mono people. This may be attributed to their social isolation, smaller size of their villages, less exposure to missionizing influence, and differences between their shamans and the sorcerers of the Ambryn people, plus greater freedom to use countersorcery and violence against corrupt shamans.

Psychological Consequences of Sorcery: Evil By Any Other Name

Although no usable data on psychiatric disorders are available for Melanesia, evidence is strong that decisions, mass hysteria, and a form of maniacal behavior—running *amok*—can be laid to sorcery fears, especially the latter. *Amok*, while commonly identified with Malaysian peoples, nevertheless occurred in New Guinea and Papua (Burton-Bradley, 1968; Langness, 1965).

Running *amok* has been described as an episodic outburst accompanied by homicidal threats and/or physical attacks on others, for no apparent cause. Typically, if I may use the word, the amokee ran through a village, shouting or chanting, destroying property, either threatening or actually attacking those in his way with a spear or jungle knife. Most persons in the vicinity, where they could, fled or avoided the *amok* driven individual. In some instances he was subdued or even killed by those he confronted.

Fortune (1932, p. 163), who encountered *amok* several times while working on Dobu, was among the first to posit sorcery fears as its cause:

> I would be inclined to connect running amok, which is
> a well known occurrence and which I encountered three
> times during my stay, with the state of mind engendered
> by witchcraft and sorcery.

Like Fortune, Young found reason to link madness, mass hysteria, and *amok* behavior with sorcery fears, a connection made explicit by his Kalauna informants. The *amok* behavior, *kwava*, spontaneously appeared as a temporary fit of frenzy and violence, in the course of which the person involved brandished weapons, chanted war spells, and ran shouting through the village, chopping at parts of houses and lunging viciously at occupants.

Those who suffered *kwava* blamed their actions on sorcerers, who, they said, "spoiled their minds" or "sent spirits to possess them." In one case the amokee threatened to spear a notorious sorcerer, muttering that "it was wartime" when sorcerers were fair game for warriors. In so doing the amokee "spoke for them all," saying in public what few even dared to say in private (Young, p. 135).

Amok as Culture Bound

Young edges towards clinical psychiatry when he refers to *amok* as a "syndrome," combining superficial cordiality masking private fears and hatreds with an almost unrelieved state of subconscious stress. Psychiatrists have found *amok* cases to be "stumbling blocks" in efforts to apply to it accepted diagnostic categories.

The best they can manage has been to append "culture bound" to their speculative syndromes. *Kwava* apparently means madness to Kalauna natives, who despite its dramatic affect nevertheless normalized *amok* as an acceptable and understandable response to intolerable conditions and feelings. The more profound meaning of *amok* lay in its cultural antecedents, driving Hindu warfare and Malay piracy.

Burton-Bradley (1968) is one of the few writers to see past attempts at psychiatric definitions, being impressed by Van Wulfften-Palthe's (1933) concise formulation of *amok* as a standardized form of emotional release, recognized as such by the community, and expected of an individual placed in an intolerably embarrassing or shameful situation. Weidman and Sussex (1971) have highlighted the place of shame in the *amok* reaction.

Sorcery fears alone may not directly cause *amok* so much as to precipitate it. The fact that amokees tend to be young to middle aged suggests that cultural stresses associated with gender conflict and socioeconomic failures combined as influences in their behavior; such things as marital dissension, gambling losses, public arguments, social isolation, and alcohol intoxication all figured in their stress.

Soldiers in Laos externalized their psychological conflicts by exploding grenades in public places. This could be a form of victimage or a statement, within a cultural tradition, that combined homicidal furor with suicidal action literally destroying the physical basis of self and other (Westermeyer, 1973).

Whether running *amok* served as social control by altering the social situation of the individual after the event is problematical. For the Laotian grenade user the answer is that little if any meaningful change came about other than regrettable deaths. In villages of Sri Lanka those running *amok* were bound and subjected to rituals exorcising the devil believed to cause their behavior. Whether such rituals are a helpful change in the individual's life or life situation is not told to us.

However, on the Island of Tikopia we find evidence that suicide attempts (of less than 100% lethal probability) on the part of women who impulsively swam out to sea did resolve status conflicts by their disclosure and reassessment of the values involved by kin and community—and the same for men who took long sea voyages single-handedly in canoes, and who sometimes returned as heroes (Firth, 1981). While such behaviors were definable as deviant, their implicitly heroic quality placed them beyond morality with respect to social control.

Evil, Legend, and Myths

It remains to inquire as to what further light can be shed on evil in Melanesian societies by the existential beliefs and epistemologies that enter into daily actions and lives of their peoples. For a more precise delimitation of an otherwise murky area, help is at hand in the introduction to a survey of religions by Lawrence and Meggitt (1965). This centers on assumptions about the total environment of these societies in explanatory myths of their origin and phenomena of a "marvelous character" (p. 262). From these came authority for beliefs and practices, based on the power of words and their specific combinations as receptacles of power.

Going beyond this formal definition to analysis is no easy task since, as I noted earlier in a brief discussion of myths, their meanings are elusive due to lack of coherent frameworks from one locality to another, and also due to the aoristic "time belong story" disregard of past, present, and future time categories. Young (1983) in considerable part overcomes this problem with his study of legendary figures of Lulauville on Goodenough Island, Papua, fleshing out the ethnography of Massim originally known in writings of Malinowski and Fortune.

The study of six such individuals, one entirely composed by a number of myth versions, the others essentially based on legendary accounts, greatly enlarges extant knowledge of the lives of Melanesian Big Men. Their personal conflicts and intro-jected social stresses acquire a larger meaning from the native term *umwewe*, signifying the plight of a person caught in the strands of lawyer cane, whose coils grow with strugle to free one's self from them. The metaphor reflects major intrapsychic perturbations derived from ecological and cultural conflicts that "celebrated abundance of food and those who provide it, but simultaneously derogates them by devious means of institutional envy" (p. 166).

Or, *umwewe* put in another way: "The covert theme of the myth [The Bones of Iyahalina] is the inadvertent loss of food counterpointed by the resolute loss of and regaining the capacity to eat" (p. 183). Or, "the message of Kuiviviole myth . . . as a notational contradiction . . . on the one hand 'food is good to eat' but on the other, 'it is good not to eat.'"

Beyond these cross-purpose cultural themes, *umwewe*, as a drive to transcendence on the "edge of morality," rose or fell short due to situational factors, such as the low ranking of the Big Man's agnatic group, lack of daughters to exchange in building a power base, possession of intimidating oratorical powers, willingness to use physical abuse, and official recognition, i.e., as a policeman.

Big-men in Kalauna, in legend and myth, directed their magical powers to environment control, generally tabooing consumption for the common good but also at times malevolently causing floods and drought. They were capable of invoking the "totally unmitigated evil" of *toof a*—the "sorcery of gluttony"—causing individuals to eat continuously without quelling their hunger, eventually being driven to scavenging and starvation in the bush (p. 132ff.).

Evil and Ethos

Another level of analysis of evil, less ecologically oriented, possibly more profound or more generalizable to Melanesian societies, is proposed by Schwartz (1973), who favors the concept of a paranoid ethos for understanding the impact of cultures on behavior. Although he employs the term advisedly, it is difficult to escape its reductionist implications.

I believe that a simpler conception, more directly aimed at the interpersonal nature of Melanesian social life, serves analysis better than that of paranoid ethos. I refer to the attenuation of trust which faults the purposes of equivalence in interindividual interaction due to impending warfare, feuding, cannibalism, gender conflict, and the duplicity that marked the behavior of Big-men driven by competitive excess to covert uses of homicide and sorcery.

My empirical referents for attenuated trust in Melanesian societies are inferred from scattered references to "sympathy groups" and to "security groups," also gleaned from a legendary passage about one Kalauna Big-man, "An incorrigible monster" responsible for "countermanding sitting circles" that led to the dispersal of social life by pushing people into the wilderness (Young, 1983, p. 98). These oblique allusions suggest to me that groups Western sociologists have defined as relatively fixed or permanent primary groups, are for Melanesians those informally organized for limited kinds of action, such as work in the sago camp or the garden house (Schliefflin, 1976, p. 132).

To rest my case on these few bits of evidence courts eyebrow lifting if not disdain among more hard-nosed scholars, even though responsibility for the deficiency of data may properly belong with ethnographers in Melanesia, who have reported very little about intraclan social interaction. Fortunately, a quick fix for my problem came to light in a biographical account obtained by a worker in the Solomon Islands (Elota, 1983, pp. 64ff.).

As I move to paraphrase his findings I immediately recognize that the term security ties is a much better concept than security groups to capture the contingent nature of interindividual interaction within the clan and that between the clan and the individual. The associated variations come into view most clearly in reactions to delicts, such as adultery, incest, or the seduction of a nubile girl of one clan by a man from a different clan:

> According to the kindred principle, each individual is the center of a *unique circle of relatives*. Two clan "brothers," even first cousins, are related through their mothers to two different maternal clans; and are also related to different clans through their paternal and maternal grandmothers. Thus if you are a fugitive, your maternal uncle and his clan are obliged to offer you refuge or to avenge your death . . . from these two principles derive the potential course and chain of blood feuds.
>
> The possible consequences of these bonds are that a girl made pregnant might either be taken off to be

married by the man, or if this was not possible she would be immediately killed by her closest male relative.

However, the ideal target was the seducer. His clan might deliver him up to the girl's clan to be killed, or another clan member might be turned over in his place. But the seducer's clan, if strong, might defend him, or his second line of relatives might take on the task.

Confronted by such resistance, the girl's clan might muster supporters to try to kill the seducer, or his immediate brother or sister, or they could put up a bounty such as pigs and other valuables—the larger the bounty the greater the prestige accruing to the clan setting it.

An outsider, such as a professional bounty hunter, a *lamo*, might kill the man at risk and claim the bounty, or his own clan might kill him on legitimate grounds that he put them all in jeopardy.

Quite often persons in the clan targeted for vengeance would either kill one of their own members or offer him up to be killed, done to collect the bounty or because he endangered them all. Such victims were persons considered to be expendable, such as an irresponsible pig thief, or one who violated ritual, or a lazy girl who polluted her menfolk, or "hangers on" without any ties within their groups.

Such contingent and variable outcomes of interclan conflict reveal the extent to which feuding and "clan politics" were interrelated, as well as illuminating the social control process by which deviant or undesirable persons were eliminated from close-bound corporate groups. As I have tried to show, this was by no means a simple or predictable set of actions.

The conspicuous influence of feuding, vengeance, and sorcery in Melanesian societies marks them as historical anomalies that substantiate Hobbs' dour premise about the brutality and nastiness of very early human life (supra 144). It is neither arrogant nor ethnocentric to speak of them as precivilized in the sense that trust, along with civility and amity, were in short supply among them, being subordinated to the avoidance of risks and dangers to life and well-being both within and outside social groups.

Melanesians are relatively unrestrained in displaying anger and hostility and, far from disapproving of them, see them as a way of initiating and sustaining social interaction.[6]

It is significant that Melanesians often had to initiate interaction with people who shortly before had been their enemies and the objects of feud. Hence the labile nature of their emotions was implicit in the patterns of reciprocity requiring partners for trade and women for marriage from erstwhile enemy tribes.

Whether, as Gouldner (1960) insisted, reciprocity is a universal norm, is debatable, but we can agree with his assertion that it serves as a "starting mechanism" for interaction and tenuous bonding found in exchange rivalry between Melanesians. Whether reciprocity had a stabilizing effect on the societies involved also is questionable largely because of the overriding cultural dilemmas about the growing, use, and consumption of food. Also there was little in the way of organized society to stabilize, given the lack of control over interpersonal violence and tyranny of leaders. Where shaming was inappropriate there remained sorcery—the ultimate evil.

A Concluding Comparative Note

Melanesians in many but not all tribes turned to violence to avenge disability and deaths they believed resulted from malicious motives behind the use of sorcery. Yet when pressed for explanations, some justified sorcery and the havoc it caused as being necessary for purposes of social control and order. At the same time their actions conveyed the low or indeterminate value placed on lives of human beings, especially those outside of their immediate security circle.

The high value placed on equivalence in Melanesian culture ran contrary to the competition for status it engendered, by combining economic distribution with specific interpersonal relationships of trading partners. This made attempts to maintain

---

6. For discussion of the conscious awareness of differing emotional states among the Llongots in the Philippines see Rosaldo, 1980; the Llongots appeared to be ambivalent about anger but happy when it led to meaningful expression of its underlying energy such as in successful head hunting (Rosaldo, 1983).

equivalence highly tenuous and distorted the significance of exchange, which was reflected in the use of shell money, the size of yams, and the numbers of pigs involved. Differences thus established became an historical basis for invidious comparisons on subsequent occasions, such as festivals, feasts, and dances.

The discontinuity of cultural values in Melanesian societies rested on a structure of age grading, segregation by age and sex, and avoidance. Socialization of males, beginning with their isolation in men's houses at an early age, and induction into a warrior's role likely proved traumatic and productive of anxiety about conformity with the masculinity values associated with the role.

7

Conclusion

Writing about evil while adhering to the method of science is no easy task, for the simple reason that evil is a mystical idea that loses an important part of its meaning when it is defined solely as an objective phenomenon. To do so omits a subjective element having to do with special feelings and emotions that defy generalization. These cannot be captured by defining evil as harm because harm is defined as evil, leaving a tautology, which is rejected by scientists, who insist on defining a phenomenon in terms of its operations.

Bridging the gap between the mystical and the real is helped by noting William James' concept of religious experience as ineffable, which can only be expressed by passive terms such as awe or reverence. In contrast, evil, while it is a variety of mystical experience, is active not passive; its dominant emotion is fear rising to panic and an urgent demand for action.

This occurs when the premonitory emotions of evil experienced by individuals are transformed into a collective expression through a process of social interaction. This process is one of contested meanings and of emergent consensus. It is influenced by fixed background factors as well as by problematic foreground factors. Among the former are nighttime fears derived from evolutionary memories, which can be observed in small children. Later their fear of the dark generalizes to the color black as a premonitor of evil, which, along with red, signals danger.

The folk recognition of the evil eye, conveyed by overgazing, along with negative charisma, illustrates the play of foreground factors in the perception of evil. Cultures "exploit" such factors;

but more particularly, groups or individuals do so. Exploitation ranges from modern films made to horrify adolescent movie-goers to the conjurations of sorcerers, who wear black clothing, roam the night, and deliver evil incantations and potions to others.

As I explained in the preface of my book, its subject matter evolved from a number of sources and finally came to rest on the topics of witchcraft and sorcery, which flourished in Africa and in Melanesia. Unfortunately the resting place is a shaky one inasmuch as no agreement exists as to the meanings of sorcery and witchcraft, and some writers use them interchangeably.

One solution to the confusion of the terms is to subsume them under the concept of magic, or to follow Kluckhohn, who distinguished different kinds of witchcraft as forms of wizardry. Another solution for the inconsistent use of the concepts of witchcraft and sorcery is to speak, write, or think of the three terms as the several ways in which power over others is exercised, and becomes a means of social control. An issue growing out of this is whether such means of social control is sufficiently regularized to consider it to be legal control.

Another line that leads out of the confusion between witch-craft and sorcery lies in use of the sociological term status. By this token witches have only adventitious or putative status, socially created by suspicion, blame, and the potential for collec-tive attack. These vary with community fears and are in turn influenced by changing socioeconomic conditions.

Viewed sociologically, sorcerers have an established status, albeit a marginal one; they are socially accepted specialists who live by exploiting the fears of others in the community. It is the sense of being exploited that generates distrust of the sorcerer and the possibility of retaliation, which, however, he minimizes by distancing himself from others.

The Witch Hunt as Social Control

Witch hunts were collective movements to control witches and witchcraft, and were largely confined to Africa. They had cult-like features but differed from cargo cults found in Melanesia. As forms of social control they aimed at inducing local peoples to give up their evil practices. This was done by harrassment and sometimes the execution of the supposed "witches." The forms that the witch hunt took were influenced by the authority of native monarchs and restricted by the policies of colonial administrators in Africa. In New Guinea and Papua, where colonialism came late and where sorcery was available to all, no witch hunts materialized; at most cargo cults there resembled witch hunts in regard to the extraction of money by leaders from their followers.

Conclusions about leadership in Melanesian societies are necessarily tentative and subject to exceptions. It was affected by the ubiquitous competition for status among followers as well as among leaders. At the same time this motivation to excel was counterbalanced by allegiance to the values of equivalence. These values emerged or were satisfied in translocal gift exchanges around which socioeconomic life was organized.

Competition of the sort attributed to Melanesians was charged with emotions of anger and distrust, whose expression did not typically precipitate conflict but rather became a stimulus to remedial gift giving. Here one sees a reflection of the stark differences between Southeast Asian cultures and those of the West. Thus for many Melanesian cultures emotions followed a categorically different pattern than in Western cultures. For people of these cultures anger, hatred, and distrust were an integral part of ordinary, recurrent social relationships as well as a means to initiate such relationships. Civility and amity stood low in the scale of Melanesian values, removed by many centuries from the culture of civility that emerged in eighteenth-century Europe. Savagery was far from being a mere state of unenlightenment for Melanesians; rather it had features of cultlike ecstasy.

The values pertaining to this distinctive savagery were those of the warrior class, whose intermittent satisfaction fluctuated with skirmishing, raiding, and warfare. The shifting periods of warfare and quiescence gave rise to alternating patterns of indulgence in violence, killing, and destruction of enemy houses, trees and gardens, followed by uneasy peace. The labile nature of the accompanying emotions may be regarded as an integral part of a warfare complex whose values were maintained by the hegemony of the warrior group. The endemic nature of Melanesian warfare followed from the lack of formal means or overriding authority necessary to bring it to an end. This contrasts sharply with the already noted formality of the Japanese people, who employ linguistic forms, bowing, verbal apologies, and carefully segregated social relationships to control conflict.

One must acknowledge that patterns of intermittent warfare did not hold for all Melanesian tribes. There were those in which warfare was persistent. Information is not available as to whether individual competition and rivalry were present in societies organized for continuous war making. However, there is evidence that the incidence of sorcery was much lower in societies with martial cultures than in those that periodically resumed social contacts with their erstwhile enemies. The greater reliance on sorcery for purposes of social control occurred more frequently in societies whose members interacted with former foes.

There were Melanesian societies that did not rely on violence and sorcery as means of social control. A broad view indicates that shaming was more often or more widely distributed as a means of social control than any other. Whether its effects were more successful than sorcery is hard to say. However, it is clear that the effects of sorcery, according to native belief, were more fateful, since they were likely to produce disease, death, or misfortune.

Shaming depended for its success on the vulnerability of those who were shamed. This in turn depended on socialization of the child. Orphans and others missing such influence often were untouched by shaming. Migratory workers could very well outgrow sensitivity to shaming, likewise "rubbish men" who were social dropouts and who did not live by the competitive ethic.

A remarkable feature of social control found throughout the area of New Guinea and Papua was the resort to self-destructive behavior on the part of individuals who felt aggrieved by others or by their failure to meet due obligations. Such persons' responses ranged from giving away money to a kind of vengeance suicide.

Peoples of the West have some general familiarity with the traditional suicide rituals of the Japanese, so-called *hara kiri*;

but examined carefully, they differ from Melanesian shaming reactions. Melanesians inflict shame on others by turning their own anger into self-demeaning and self-destructive actions, not to erase their shame so much as to project it onto the offending others.

Suicide can have a number of different meanings even within the same culture. Melanesian self-directed destructiveness and immolation can be interpreted as a form of transcendence—a reaching for ultimate experience or a final resolution of life conflicts. The same holds for Japanese under certain circumstances, when they commit suicide, not necessarily to expunge shame but to achieve some pinnacle of ecstasy—as when teenage lovers leap into a volcano. It is shown even more graphically by a present day film, *Realm of the Senses*, in which a Japanese prostitute cuts off the genitals of her lover in the final act of a tempestuous love affair.

Japanese and Melanesian instances of transcendence underscore the many shapes that such experience takes in other cultures, from adolescent thrills felt with shoplifting to the fulminations of great leaders, who are "overcome by their belief in themselves" (Nietzsche's phrase). It is for this reason along with others that transcendence is recognized as a process rather than as a state of a condition. Furthermore, whether transcendence is evil depends on the meaning it acquires in social interaction.

In broad perspective it is unfortunate but true that many questions can be raised about aspects of Melanesian cultures for which answers cannot be found in published ethnographies of the area. This does not fault the field workers who gathered the available knowledge. Rather it is a commentary on the impossible task before them, faced as they have been with the diversity of cultures to record and the rapid rate at which they changed after World War II contacts.

Fairness and the pleasure from the opportunity to read their accounts leads me to applaud the richness and intriguing variety of the ethnographers' data that are available. On the down side I must say or admit that their reluctance or failure to make cross-cultural comparisons was a disappointment. Conversations with some of my anthropological friends suggest that this may have been naiveté on my part. On the other hand it may harken back to the time when I and a few others believed that combined training in the fields of sociology and anthropology was, as is now said, "the way to go."

References

1966. Aberle, David. "Magical Phenomena and Power." *Southwestern Journal of Anthropology* 22: 221–242.

1935. "An African Explains Witchcraft." *Africa* 8: 504–59.

1970. Ardener, Edwin. "Witchcraft, Economics, and the Continuity of Belief." In Mary Douglas, ed., *Witchcraft: Confessions and Accusations*. London: Tavistock. Pp. 141–60.

1965. Arendt, Hannah. *Eichmann in Jerusalem: A Report on the Banality of Evil*. London: Penguin Books.

1917. Arensberg, Conrad. *The Irish Countryman*. New York: Press.

1976. Argyle, Michael and Cook, Mark. *Gaze and Mutual Gaze*. London: Cambridge University Press.

1982. Aubert, Vilhelm. *The Hidden Society*. New Brunswick, NJ: Transaction Books.

1962. Barnes, J. A. "African Models in the New Guinea Highlands." *Man* 62: 5–9.

1971. Bellah, Robert. "Evil and the American Ethos." In *Sanctions for Evil*.

1934. Benedict, Ruth. *Patterns of Culture*. Boston: Houghton Mifflin.

1971. Berger, Bennet. *Looking for America: Essays on Youth, Suburbia and Other American Obsessions*. Englewood Cliffs: Prentice Hall.

1962. Berndt. *Excess and Restraint Among Highland New Guinea People*. Cambridge: Cambridge Universiy Press.

1983. Black, Donald. "Crime as Social Control." In *Toward a General Theory of Social Control. Volume 2: Selected Problems*. Orlando: Academic Press. Pp. 1–27.

1962. Bloomhill, Greta. *Witchcraft in Africa*. Capetown: Howard Timmins.

165

1580. Bodin, Jean. *De La Demonomania des Sorciers*. Paris: Du Puys.

1964. Bohannon, Laura (Eleanor Smith Bowen). *Return to Laughter*. New York: Anchor Books.

1987. Bowden, Ross. "Sorcery, Illness, and Social Control in Kwoma." In Michele Stephen, ed., *Sorcerer and Witch in Melanesia*. New Brunswick, NJ: Rutgers University Press. Pp. 183–210.

1985. Boyle, Richard P. "Dark Side of Mead: Neuropsychological Foundation for Intermediate Experience and Mystical Consciousness." *Studies in Symbolic Interaction* 6: 59–78.

1970. Brain, C. F. "New Finds at Swartkans Australopecine Site." *Nature* 225: 1112–1119.

1970. Brain, Robert. "Child Witches." In Mary Douglas, ed. *Witchcraft: Confessions and Accusations*. London: Tavistock. Pp. 161–79.

1970. Briggs, Jean L. *Never in Anger: Portrait of an Eskimo Family*. Cambridge: Cambridge University Press.

1969. Brown, B. J. ed. *Fashion of Law in New Guinea*. Sydney: Butterworths.

1952. Brown, Radcliffe. *Structure and Function in Primitive Society: Essays and Addresses*. London: Cohen and West.

1965–66. Burridge, K. O. L. "Tangu Political Relations." *Anthropological Forum* 1: 393–411.

1975. ———. "The Melanesian Manager." In J. H. M. Beattie and R. G. Lienhardt, eds. *Studies in Social Anthropology: Essays in Honour of E. E. Evans-Pritchard*. Oxford: Clarendon Press.

1960. Burton-Bradley, B. G. "The Amok Syndrome In Papua and New Guinea." *Medical Journal of Australia*. 1, 7 (February 17): 252–56.

1969. Bushnell, Horace. *Moral Uses of Dark Things*. New York: C. Scribner.

1963. Buxton, Jean. "Mandari Witchcraft." In John Middleton and Edward H. Winter, eds. *Witchcraft and Sorcery in East Africa*. London: Routledge and Kegan Paul. Pp. 99–121.

1961. Chowning, Ann. "Amok and Aggression in the D'Entrecasteaux." *Proceedings of the Annual Meeting of the American Ethnological Society* (Spring). Seattle, WA: University of Washington Press. Pp. 78–83.

1974. ———. "Disputing in Two West New Britain Societies." In A. L. Epstein, ed. *Contention and Dispute: Aspects of Law and Social Control in Melanesia.* Canberra: Australian National University Press. Pp. 152–97.

1970. Cohen, Albert. "Multiple Factor Analysis." In Marvin Wolfgang, et al., eds. *The Sociology of Crime.* New York: Wiley. Pp. 123–26.

1975. Cohn, Norman. *Europe's Inner Demons: An Inquiry Inspired by the Great Witch Hunts.* New York: Basic Books.

1953. Colson, Elizabeth F. "Social Control and Vengeance in Plateau Tonga Society." *Africa* 23: 199–212.

1969. Coser, Lewis. "The Visibility of Evil." *Journal of Social Issues* 25: 101–109.

1972. Cottrell, William F. *Technology, Man and Progress.* Columbus, OH: Merrill.

1970. Counts, D. R. and D. F. Counts. "The Vula of Kalai: A Primitive Currency with a Commercial Use." *Oceania* 51,2: 90–105.

1967. Crawford, J. R. *Witchcraft and Sorcery in Rhodesia.* London: Oxford University Press.

1990. Crowdog, Mary and Erdoes, Richard. *Lakota Woman.* New York: Harper.

1986. Davis, Murray. "That's Classic! The Phenomenology of Successful Social Theories." *Philosophy of the Social Sciences* 16: 285–86.

1979. Dort, Bernard. "Genet: The Struggle with Theater." Translated by Ruth Goldfarb. In Peter Brooks and Joseph Halpern, eds. *Genet: A Collection of Critical Essays.* Englewood Cliffs, NJ: Prentice-Hall. Pp. 114–28.

1970. Douglas, Mary. "Introduction." In Mary Douglas, ed. *Witchcraft: Confessions and Accusations.* London: Tavistock. Pp. xiii–xxxviii.

1963. ———. "Techniques of Sorcery Control in Central Africa." In John Middleton and Edward H. Winter, eds. *Witchcraft and Sorcery in East Africa.* London: Routledge and Kegan Paul. Pp. 123–41.

1971. Duster, Troy. "Conditions for a Guilt Free Massacre." In Nevitt Sanford, Craig Comstock, et al., eds. *Sanctions for*

Evil: Sources of Social Destructiveness. Boston: Beacon Press. Pp. 25–36.

1992. Edgerton, Robert B. *Sick Societies: Challenging the Myth of Primitive Harmony*. New York: Free Press.

1983. Elota. *Elota's Story: The Life and Times of a Solomon Islands Big Man*. Ed. Robert M. Keesing. New York: Holt, Rinehart, and Winston.

1977. Emerson, Robert and Sheldon Messinger. "The Micropolitics of Trouble." *Social Problems* 25: 121–32.

1974. Epstein, A. L., ed. *Contention and Dispute: Aspects of Law and Social Control in Melanesia*. Canberra: Australian National University Press.

1984. ———. *The Experience of Shame in Melanesia: An Essay in the Anthropology of Affect*. London: Royal Anthropological Institute of Great Britain and Ireland.

1966. Erikson, Kai T. *Wayward Puritans: A Study in the Sociology of Deviance*. New York: Wiley.

1953. Evans-Pritchard, E. E. "Nuer Curses and Ghostly Vengeance." *Africa* 19: 288–92.

1931. ———. "Sorcery and Native Opinion." *Africa* 4: 22–54.

1937. ———. *Witchcraft, Oracles, and Magic among the Azande*. Oxford: Clarendon Press.

1961. Firth, Raymond. "Suicide and Risk-Taking in Tikopia Society." *Psychiatry* 24,1: 1–17.

1970. Forge, J. and A. Forge. "Prestige, Influence, and Sorcery: A New Guinea Example." In Mary Douglas, ed. *Witchcraft: Confessions and Accusations*. London: Tavistock. Pp. 259–95.

1932. Fortune, Reo F. *Sorcerers of Dobu: The Social Anthropology of the Dobu Islanders of the Western Pacific*. New York: Columbia University Press.

1967. Foster, George. *Tzintzuntzan: Mexican Peasants in a Changing World*. Boston: Little Brown.

1967. Fox, J. Robin. "Witchcraft and Clanship in Cochiti Therapy." In *Magic, Witchcraft, and Curing*. Ed. John Middleton. Garden City, New York: The Natural History Press. Pp. 255–84.

1956. Garfinkel, Harold. "Conditions of Successful Degradation Ceremonies." *American Journal of Sociology* 61,5: 420–424.

1961. Gaster, Theodore H. ed. Frazer, Sir James George. *The New Golden Bough*. New York: Anchor Books.

1930. Gayton, A. H. *Yokuts-Mono Chiefs and Shamans*. Berkeley and Los Angeles: University of California Publications in American Archeology and Ethnology.

1934. Gillin, John. "Crime and Punishment Among the Barama River Caribs." *American Anthropologist* 36: 331–44.

1969. Glasse, R.M. "Revenge and Redress Among the Huli." *Mankind* 5: 273–89.

1972. Gluckman, Max, ed. *The Allocation of Responsibility*. Manchester: Manchester University Press.

1956. ———. *Custom and Conflict in Africa*. Oxford: Blackwell.

1972. ———. "Moral Curses: Magical and Secular Solutions." In *The Allocation of Responsibility*. Ed. Max Gluckman. Manchester: Manchester University Press. Pp. 1–50.

1965. ———. *The Ideas in Barotse Jurisprudence*. New Haven: Yale University Press.

1965. ———. *Politics, Law and Ritual in Tribal Society*. Chicago: Aldine.

1963. Goffman, Erving. "On Facework." In Erving Goffman, *Interaction Ritual: Essays on Face-to-Face Behavior*. New York: Anchor Books. Pp. 5–45.

1970. Goody, Esther. "Legitimate and Illegitimate Aggression in a West African State." In Mary Douglas, ed. *Witchcraft: Confessions and Accusations*. London: Tavistock. Pp. 207–44.

1960. Gouldner, Alvin. "The Norm of Reciprocity: A Preliminary Statement." *American Sociological Review* 25,2: 161–78.

1984. Graubard, Marc. *Witchcraft and the Nature of Man*. Philadelphia, PA: University of Pennsylvania Press.

1963. Gray, Robert F. "Some Structural Aspects of Sorcery and Witchcraft." In John Middleton and E. H. Winter, eds. *Witchcraft and Sorcery in East Africa*. New York: Praeger. Pp. 143–73.

1974. Greeley, Andrew M. and William McReady. "Some Notes on the Sociological Study of Mysticism." In Edward Tiryakian, ed., *On the Margin of the Visible*. New York: Wiley.

1991. Griffin, David Ray. *Evil Revisited: Responses and Reconsiderations*. New York: SUNY Press.

1963. Gulliver, P. H. *Social Control in an African Society.* Boston: Boston University Press.

1988. Gusfield, Joseph. "Constructing Ownership of Social Problems: Fun and Profit in the Welfare State." *Social Problems* 36,5 (December): 431–41.

1981. ———. *The Culture of Public Problems.* Chicago: University of Chicago Press.

1981. ———. "Moral Passage: The Symbolic Process in the Public Designation of Deviance." *Social Problems* 15 (Fall): 175–88.

1935. Hall, Jerome. *Theft, Law, and Society.* Boston: Little, Brown

1977. Hallpike, C. R. *Bloodshed and Vengeance in the Papuan Mountains: The Generation of Conflict in Tuade Society.* Oxford: Clarendon Press.

1932. Hamilton, Alexander H. "Institutions." *Encyclopedia of the Social Sciences.* London: MacmillanCo. Volume 8: 84–89.

1924. Hartland, E.S. *Primitive Law.* London: Methuen and Co.

1954. Hartung, Frank E. "Cultural Relativity and Moral Judgment." *Philosophy of Science* 21 (April): 118–26.

1970. Harwood, Alan. *Witchcraft: Sorcery and Social Categories Among the Safwa.* London: Oxford University Press.

1971. Hau'ofa, Epeli. *Mekeo Chieftainship. Journal of the Polynesian Society* 51. Pp. 152–69.

1975. Hayes, Douglas, et al. *Albion's Fatal Tree: Crime and Society in Eighteenth Century England.* New York: Pantheon Books.

1970. Henderson, L. J. *On the Social System.* Ed. Bernard Barber. Chicago: University of Chicago Press.

1937. Herskovits, Melville J. *Life in Haitian Valley.* New York: Knopf.

1973. Hertz, Robert. "The Preeminence of the Right Hand: A Study in Religious Polarity." In Rodney Needham, ed., *Right and Left: Essays on Dual Symbolic Classification.* Chicago: University of Chicago Press. Pp. 3–31.

1973. Hirschi, Travis. "Procedural Rules and the Study of Social Problems." *Social Problems* 21 (Fall): 159–73.

1992. Hirts, Frank. *Social Policy Options in Mozambique—A Preliminary Assessment.* Maputo, Tanzania: German Agency for Technical Cooperation (GTZ).

1968. Hoebel, E. Adamson. *The Law of Primitive Man*. New York: Atheneum.

1934. Hogbin, H. Ian. "Culture Change in the Solomon Islands: Report of Fieldwork on Guadalcanal and Malaita." *Oceania* 4: 233–67.

1945. ———. "Notes and Instructions to Native Administrators in the Solomon Islands." *Oceania* 2: 174–78.

1947. ———. "Shame: A Study of Social Conformity in a New Guinea Village." *Oceania* 17,4 (June): 273–88.

1897. Holmes, Oliver Wendell. "The Path of the Law." *Harvard Law Review* 10,8 (March 25): 457–78.

1979. Horton, Robin. "Material Object Language and Theoretical Language: Towards a Strawsonian Sociology of Thought." In S. C. Brown, ed. *Philosophical Disputes in the Social Sciences*. London: Harvester Press. Pp. 197–224.

1971. Hughes, Everett. *The Sociological Eye: Selected Papers*. Chicago: Aldine.

1962. ———. "Good People and Dirty Work." *Social Problems* 10,1 (Summer): 3–11.

1990. Hunter, Albert, ed. *The Rhetoric of Social Research*. New Brunswick, NJ: Rutgers University Press.

1987. Ito, Karen. "Emotions, Proper Behavior (Hana Pono) and Hawaiian Concepts of Self, Person and the Individual." In Albert B. Robillard and Anthony J. Marselle, eds. *Contemporary Issues in Mental Health Research in the Pacific Islands*. Honolulu, HI: Social Science Research Institute, University of Hawaii. Pp. 45–71.

1985. James, William. *The Varieties of Religious Experience*. Cambridge: Harvard University Press.

1951. Jones, G. *Basutoland Medicine Murder: A Report on the Recent Outbreak of Diretto Murders in Basutoland*. London: HMSO.

1936. Junod, Henri. "Notes on the Ethnological Situation in Portugese East Africa on the South of the Zambesi." *Bantu Studies* 10: 293–311.

1988. Katz, Jack. *Seductions of Crime: The Moral and Sensual Attractions of Evil*. New York: Basic Books.

1972. ———. "Deviance, Charisma and Rule Defined Behavior." *Social Problems* 20,3 (Fall): 186–202.

1984. Kavolis, Vytantas. "Civilizational Models of Evil." In Marie C. Nelson and Michael Eigen, eds. *Evil, Self, and Culture.* New York: Human Sciences. Pp. 17–35.

1967. Kennedy, John G. "Psychological and Sociological Explanations of Witchcraft." *Man* 2: 218.

1972. Kent, Janet. *The Solomon Islands.* Harrisburg, PA: Stackpole Books.

1982. Kiernan, J. P. "The 'Problem of Evil' in the Context of Ancestral Intervention in the Affairs of the Living in Africa." *Man* 17: 287–301.

1906. Kleintitschen, August. *Die Kustenbewohner der Gazellehalbinsel.* Hiltrup bei Munster: Herz-Jesu-Missionhaus.

1955. Kluckhohn, Clyde. "Ethnical Relativity: Sic et Non." *Journal of Philosophy* 52 (November 10): 663–77.

1944. ———. *Navaho Witchcraft.* Boston: Beacon Press.

1985. Knauft, Bruce M. *Good Company and Violence: Sorcery and Social Action in a Lowland New Guinea Society.* Berkeley: University of California Press.

1990. ———. "Melanesian Warfare: A Theoretical History." *Oceania* 60: 250–311.

N. D. Kove. Political Organization. Unpublished manuscript.

1962. Kuhn, Thomas. *The Structure of Scientific Revolutions.* Chicago: University of Chicago Press.

1988. Kumagai, Hisa. "*Ki*: The Fervor of Vitality in the Subjective Self." *Symbolic Interaction* 11,2 (Fall): 175–90.

1963. La Fontaine, Jean. "Witchcraft in Bugisu." In John Middleton and Edward H. Winter, eds. *Witchcraft and Sorcery in East Africa.* London: Routledge and Kegan Paul. Pp. 187–220.

1965. Langness, L. L. "Hysterical Psychosis in the New Guinea Highlands: A Bena Bena Example." *Psychiatry* 28: 258–77.

1965. ———. *The Life History in Anthropological Science.* New York: Holt, Rinehart, and Winston.

1938. La Piere, Richard T. *Collective Behavior.* New York: McGraw-Hill.

1989. Laub, Ervin. *The Roots of Evil.* New York: Cambridge University Press.

1965. Lawrence, P. and M. J. Meggit, Eds. *Gods, Ghost and More in Melanesia.* Melbourne, Oxford.

1964. ———. *Road Belong Cargo: Study of Cargo Cults in the South Madang District, New Guinea.* Manchester: Manchester University Press.

1969. ———. "The State versus Stateless Society in Papua and New Guinea." In B. J. Brown, ed., *Fashion of Law in New Guinea.* Sydney: Butterworths.

1981. Lederman, Rena. "Sorcery and Social Change in Mendi." *Social Analysis* 8 (November): 15–27.

1972. Lemert, Edwin M. "The Behavior of the Systematic Forger." In Edwin M. Lemert, *Human Deviance, Social Problems, and Social Control.* Englewood Cliffs, NJ: Prentice-Hall. Pp. 150–61.

1981. ———. "Issues in the Study of Deviance." *Sociological Quarterly* 22 (Spring): 285–305.

1972. ———. *Human Deviance, Social Problems, and Social Control.* 2nd ed. Englewood Cliffs NJ: Prentice-Hall.

1972. ———. Koni, Kona, Kava: The Secular Use of Kava with Reference to Tonga in Human Deviance, Social Problems and Social Control.

1942. ———. "The Folkways and Social Control." *American Sociological Review* 7,3 (June): 34–45.

1964/1967. ———. "Forms and Pathology of Drinking in Three Polynesian Societies." *American Anthropologist* 66: 361–74.

1972. ———. "Role Enactment, Self, and Identity in the Systematic Check forger." In Edwin M. Lemert, *Human Deviance, Social Problems, and Social Control.* 2nd ed. Englewood Cliffs, NJ: Prentice-Hall. Pp. 162–82.

1963. Le Vine, Robert. "Witchcraft and Sorcery in a Gusii Community." In John Middleton and Edward H. Winter, eds. *Witchcraft and Sorcery in East Africa.* London: Routledge and Kegan Paul. Pp. 221–55.

1979. Lindenbaum, Shirley. *Kuru Sorcery: Disease and Danger in the New Guinea Highlands.* Palo Alto: Mayfield.

1987. Lindstrom, Lamont, ed. *Drugs in Western Pacific Societies.* Lanham, MD: University Press of America.

1954. Linton, Ralph. "The Problem of Universal Values." In Robert F. Spencer, ed., *Method and Perspectives in Anthropology.* Minneapolis, MN: University of Minnesota Press. Pp. 150–52, 166.

1936. ———. *The Study of Man*. New York: Appleton-Century-Crofts.

1952. ———. "Universal Moral Principles: An Anthropological View." In Ruth Anshen, ed., *Moral Principles of Action: Man's Ethical Imperative*. New York: Harper. Pp. 645–60.

1925. Lippmann, Walter. *Public Opinion*. New York: Macmillan.

1940. Llewellyn, Karl. "The Normative, The Legal, and the Law-Jobs: The Problem of the Juristic Method." *Yale Law Journal* 49,8 (June): 1355–400.

1941. Llewellyn, Karl and E. Adamson Hoebel. *The Cheyenne Way*. Norman, OK: University of Oklahoma Press.

1978. Lyman, Stanford. *The Seven Deadly Sins: Society and Evil*. New York: St. Martins Press.

1989. Lyman, Stanford and Marvin Scott. *Sociology of the Absurd*. Dix Hills, NJ: General Hall.

1926. Malinowski, Bronislaw. *Crime and Custom in Savage Society*. New York: Harcourt, Brace, and Co.

1959. Marsack, C. C. "Provocation in Trials for Murder." *Criminal Law Review*: 681–744.

1967. Marwick, M. G. "The Sociology of Sorcery in a Central African Tribe." In John Middleton, ed. *Magic, Witchcraft, and Curing*. Garden City, NY: Natural History Press. Pp. 101–26.

1964. ———. "Witchcraft as a Social Strain Gauge." *Australian Journal of Science* 26: 263–68.

1969. Matza, David. *Becoming Deviant*. Englewood Cliffs, NJ: Prentice Hall.

1956. Mead, George Herbert. *On Social Psychology: Selected Papers*. Ed. Anselm Strauss. Chicago: University of Chicago Press.

1961. Mead, Margaret. *Coming of Age In Samoa*. New York: Morrow.

1949. Merton, Robert. *Social Theory and Social Structure*. Glencoe, IL: The Free Press.

1962. Messinger, Sheldon. "Life as a Theater: Some Notes on the Dramaturgic Approach to Reality." *Sociometry* 25: 98–110.

1954. Middleton, John. "Some Social Aspects of Lugbara Myth." *Africa* 24 (July): 189–99.

1965. Mitchell, J. Clyde. "The Meaning of Misfortune for Urban Africans." In M. Fortes & G. Dieterlen, eds. *African Systems of Thought*. London: Oxford University Press. Pp. 192–203.

1965. Moore, Sally. "Legal Liability and Evolutionary Interpretation: Some Aspects of Liability Self-Help and Collective Responsibility." In Max Gluckman, ed. *The Allocation of Responsibility*. Manchester: Manchester University Press. Pp. 51–107.

1975. Morris, Ivan. *The Nobility of Failure: Tragic Figures in the History of Japan*. New York: Holt, Rinehart, and Winston.

1935. Nadel, S. F. "Witchcraft and Anti-Witchcraft in Nupe Society." *Africa* 8: 423–47.

1964. Nader, Laura. "An Analysis of Zapotec Law Cases." *Ethnology* 3,4: 404–19.

1967. Nash, Manning. "Witchcraft as a Social Process in a Tzetal Community." In John Middleton, ed. *Magic, Witchcraft, and Curing*. Garden City, NY: Natural History Press. Pp. 129–33.

1956. Nietzche, Friedreich. *The Birth of Tragedy and the Genealogy of Morals*. Translated by Francis Golffing. New York: Doubleday.

1934. Oberg, Kalvero. "Crime and Punishment in the Tlingit Society." *American Anthropologist* 36: 145–156.

1981. Olson, Alan M. and Leroy S. Rouner, eds. *Transcendence and the Sacred*. Notre Dame, IN: University of Notre Dame Press.

1979. Onaka. Hammod Press, Sidney.

1967. Paine, Pobert. "What Is Gossip About? An Alternative Hypothesis." *Man: The Journal of the Royal Anthropological Institute* 2: 278–85.

1963. Park, George K. "Divination and Social Context." *Journal of the Royal Anthropological Institute* 93,2: 195–209.

1985. Parkin, David. "Entitling Evil: Muslims and Non-Muslims in Coastal Kenya." In David Parkin, ed. *The Anthropology of Evil*. Oxford: Basil Blackwell. Pp. 224–43.

1927. Parsons, Elsie Clews. "Witchcraft Among the Pueblos: Indian or Spanish?" *Man* 27: 106–12, 125–8.

1974. Patterson, Mary. "Sorcery and Witchcraft in Melanesia." *Oceania* 45: 132–60.

1967. Peters, E. L. "Some Structural Aspects of Feud Among the Camel-herding Bedowin of Cyrenica." *Africa* 37: 261–82.

1964. Pitt-Rivers, Julian. "Witch and Sorcery in a Quiche Village." *Ethnology* 3: 305–28.

1983. Poole, F. J. P. "Tanam: Ideological and Sociological Configurations of 'Witchcraft' Among Bimin-Kuskusmin." *Social Analysis* 8: 58–87.

1952. Radcliffe-Brown, A. R. *Structure and Function in Primitive Society*. London: Cohen and West.

1959. Read, K. E. "Leadership and Consensus in New Guinea Society." *American Anthropologist* 61: 425–36.

1987. ———. "Morality and the Concept of the Person Among the Gahuku Gama." In John Middleton, ed., *Myth and Cosmos: Readings in Mythology and Symbolism*. New York: American Museum of Natural History. Pp. 185–229.

1959. Reay, Marie. *The Kuma: Freedom and Conformity in the New Guinea Highlands*. New Haven: Yale University Press.

1987. ———. "The Magical and Religious Foundations of New Guinea Warfare." In Michele Stephen, ed. *Sorcerer and Witch in Melanesia*. New Brunswick, NJ: Rutgers University Press.

1976. ———. "The Politics of Witch Killing." *Oceania* 47,1: 1–20.

1959. ———. "Social Control Amongst the Orakaiva." *Oceania* 24,2: 110–18.

1970. Redmayne, Alisan. "Chikanga. An African Diviner with an International Reputation." In Mary Douglas, ed. *Witchcraft: Confessions and Accusations*. London: Tavistock. Pp. 103–28.

1935. Richards, Audrey I. "A Modern Movement of Witch-Finders." *Africa* 8: 448–60.

1967. Ricouer, Paul. "Evil." *Encyclopedia of Religion*. New York: Macmillan: 199–208.

1987. ———. *The Symbolism of Evil*. Translated by E. Buchanan. Boston: Beacon Press.

1945–46. Röheim, Geza. "Yaboanie, A War God of Normanby Island." *Oceania* 16: 210–336.

1980. Rosaldo, Michelle. *Knowledge and Passion: Ilongot Notions of Self and Social Life*. Cambridge: Cambridge University Press.

1983. ———. "The Shame of Headhunters and the Autonomy of the Self." *Ethos* 11: 135–51.

1907. Ross, E. A. *Sin and Society*. New York: Houghton-Mifflin.

1961. Rotberg, Robert. *The Lenshina Movement of Northern Rhodesia*. Livingstone, Rhodesia: Rhodes Livingstone Institute.

1977. Russell, Jeffrey. *The Devil: Perceptions of Evil from Antiquity to Primitive Christianity*. Ithaca, NY: Cornell University Press. Pp. 193–226.

1974. Sack, Peter G. "The Range of Traditional Tolai Remedies." In A.L. Epstein, ed. *Contention and Dispute: Aspects of Law and Social Control in Melanesia*. Canberra: Australian National University Press. Pp. 67–92.

1963. Sahlins, Marshall. "Poor Man, Rich Man, Big Man Chief: Political Types in Melanesia and Polynesia." *Comparative Studies in Society and History* 5,3: 285–303.

1981. Sanford, John. *Evil: The Shadow Side of Reality*. New York: Crossroads Press.

1971. Sanford, Nevitt, and Craig Comstock. *Sanctions For Evil*. Boston: Beacon Press.

1972. Sansom, Basil. "When Witches Are Not Named." In Max Gluckman, *The Allocation of Responsibility*. Manchester: Manchester University Press.

1969. Sawyer, G. "Introduction." In B. J. Brown, ed. *Fashion of Law in New Guinea*. Sydney: Butterworths.

1964. Scheffler, H.W. "The Social Consequences of Peace on Choiseul Island." *Ethnology* 3: 398–403.

1976. Schieffelin, Edward L. *The Sorrow of the Lonely and the Burning of the Dancers*. New York: St. Martins Press.

1973. Schwartz, Theodore. "Cult and Context: The Paranoid Ethos in Melanesia." *Ethos* 1: 153–74.

1937. Seagle, William. *History of Law*. New York: Tudor.

1946. ———. *History of Law*. 2nd ed. New York: Tudor.

1937. ———. "Primitive Law and Professor Malinowski." *American Anthropologist* 39,2 (April–June): 275–90.

1974. Selby, Henry. *Zapotec Deviance*. Austin, TX: University of Texas Press.

1979. Shoham, S. Giora. *Salvation Through the Gutters: Deviance and Transcendence*. Washington: Hemisphere Publishing Co.

1978. Sillitoe, Paul. "Big Men and War in New Guinea." *Man* 13: 252–71.

1989. Simon, Herbert, ed. *Rhetoric in the Human Sciences.* London: Sage.

1974. Simmons, Marc. *Witchcraft in the Southwest: Spanish and Indian Supernaturalism in the Rio Grande.* Flagstaff, AZ: Northland Press.

1971. Smelser, Neil J. "Some Determinants of Destructive Behavior." In Nevitt Sanford, Craig Comstock, eds. *Sanctions of Evil: Sources of Social Destructiveness.* Pp. 15–24.

1959. Smith, Marian W. "Towards a Classification of Cult Movements." *Man* 59: 8–12.

1959. Stanner, W. E. H. "Continuity and Schism in an African Tribe: A Review." *Oceania* 29: 208–17.

1975. Steadman, Lyle. "Cannibal Witches in the Hewa." *Oceania* 46,2: 14–21.

1987. Stephen, Michele. "Master of Souls: The Mekeo Sorcerer." In Michele Stephen, ed., *Sorcerer and Witch in Melanesia.* New Brunswick, NJ: Rutgers University Press. Pp. 41–82.

N. D. Stivers, Richard. *The Concealed Rhetoric of Sociology: Social Problems as a Symbol of Evil.*

1982. ———. *Evil in Modern Myth and Ritual.* Athens, GA: University of Georgia Press.

1966. Strathern, A. "Despots and Directors in the New Guinea Highlands." *Man* (N.S.) 1: 356–67.

1982. ———. ed. *Inequality in New Guinea Society.* Cambridge: Cambridge University Press.

1971. ———. *The Rope of Moka: Big Men and Ceremonial Exchange in Mount Hagen, New Guinea.* Cambridge: Cambridge University Press.

1906. Sumner, William Graham. *The Folkways.* Boston: Ginn and Company.

1961. Tart, David. *The Kokomba of Northern Gana.* London: Oxford University Press.

1984. Taylor, Laurie. *In the Underworld.* London: Basil Blackwell.

1935. Todd, J. A. "Reddress of Wrongs in Southwest New Britain." *Oceania* 400–440.

1981. Tomkinson, Robert. "Sorcery and Social Change in Southern Ambrym, Vanatu." *Social Analysis* 8: 77–88.

1958. Toulmin, Stephen. *The Uses of Argument*. Cambridge: Cambridge University Press.

1943. Tracktenberg, Joshua. *The Devil and the Jews: The Medieval Conception of the Jew and Its Relation to Modern Antisemitism*. New Haven: Yale University Press.

1970. Turner, P. "Witchcraft and Negative Charisma." *Ethnology* 9: 360–70.

1966. Turner, Victor. "Colour Classification in Ndembu Ritual: A Problem in Primitive Classification." In Michael Banton, ed. *Anthropological Approaches to the Study of Religion*. London: Tavistock. Pp. 47–84.

1964. ———. "Witchcraft and Sorcery: Taxonomy Versus Dynamics." *Africa* 34: 314–23.

1974. Tuzin, D. F. *The Voice of Tambaran: Truth and Illusion in Illahita Arapesh Religion*. Berkeley and Los Angeles: University of California Press.

1937. Van Valkenberg, R.F. "Navaho Common Law II: Navaho Law and Justice." *Northern Arizona Museum Notes* 9: 51–54.

1933. Van Wulfften-Palthe, P. M. "Amok." *Nederlands Tijdschrift voor Geneeskunde* 7: 983.

1956. Ward, Barbara. "Some Observations on Religious Cults in Ashinti." *Africa* 26: 47–61.

1958. Weber, Max. *The Protestant Ethnic and the Spirit of Capitalism*. New York: Scribners.

1971. Weidman, H., and J. N. Sussex. "Cultural Values and Ego Functioning in Relation to the Atypical Culture Bound Reactive Syndromes." *International Journal of Social Psychiatry* 17, 2 (Spring): 83–100.

1973. Westermeyer, Joseph. "On the Epidemicity of Amok Violence." *Archives of General Psychiatry* 28,6 (June): 873–76.

1950. Whiting, Beatrice Slyth. *Paiute Sorcery*. New York: Viking Fund Publications.

1930. Williams, F. E. *Orokaiva Society*. Oxford: Clarendon Press.

1985. Willis, Roy. "Do the Fipa Have a Word for It?" David Parkin, ed., *The Anthropology of Evil*. Oxford: Basil Blackwell. Pp. 209–23.

1968. ———. "Kamcape: Anti-Sorcery Movement in South West Tanzania." *Africa* 38,1: 1–15.

1945. Wilson, Godfrey and Monica Wilson. *The Analysis of Social Change: Based on Observations in Central Africa.* Cambridge: Cambridge University Press.

1963. Winter, E. H. "The Enemy Within: Amba Witchcraft and Sociological Theory." In John Middleton and E.H. Winter, eds. *Witchcraft and Sorcery in East Africa.* London: Routledge and Kegan Paul. Pp. 277–99.

1969. Wolff, Kurt. "For a Sociology of Evil." *Journal of Social Issues.* 25, 1: 111–25.

1967. ———. "Pour une Sociologie du Mal." *L'Homme et la Societe* 4: 197–213.

1964. ———. "Note sul Profilarsi di una Nuova Scienza Sociale." *Centro Sociale* 55: 30–40.

1988. Young, Michael W., ed. *Malinowski Among the Magi: the Natives of Mailu.* London: Routledge.

1983. ———. *Magicians of Manumanua.* University of California Press.

1974. ———. *Fighting with Food.* Cambridge: Cambridge University Press.

1983. Zelenietz, Marty. "The End of Head Hunting." In Margaret Rodman and Matthew Cooper, eds., *The Pacification of Melanesia.* Ann Arbor: University of Michigan Press. Pp. 91–108.

1981. Zelenietz, Marty and Shirley Lindenbaum, eds. *Sorcery and Social Change in Melanesia.* Adelaide: Department of Anthropology, University of Adelaide.

1963. Znaniecki, Florian. *Cultural Sciences: Their Origin and Development.* Urbana, IL: University of Illinois Press.

Index